How to Read Tarot Cards

Crafted by Skriuwer

Copyright © 2024 by Skriuwer.

All rights reserved. No part of this book may be used or reproduced in any form whatsoever without written permission except in the case of brief quotations in critical articles or reviews.

For more information, contact : **kontakt@skriuwer.com** (www.skriuwer.com)

TABLE OF CONTENTS

CHAPTER 1: INTRODUCTION TO TAROT

- *What Tarot is and why people use it*
- *Basic structure of a Tarot deck*
- *Myths and truths about Tarot*

CHAPTER 2: A BRIEF HISTORY OF TAROT

- *Origins of playing cards in China and Europe*
- *How Tarot evolved from a card game*
- *Influential figures and the shift to divination*

CHAPTER 3: UNDERSTANDING THE TAROT DECK

- *Major vs. Minor Arcana overview*
- *Four suits and their elemental associations*
- *Card imagery and its role in readings*

CHAPTER 4: THE MAJOR ARCANA CARDS

- *Detailed meanings of the 22 Major Arcana*
- *"Fool's Journey" concept and life lessons*
- *How Major Arcana influences a reading*

CHAPTER 5: THE MINOR ARCANA CARDS

- *Ace to 10 in each suit and everyday matters*
- *Identifying patterns and numerical progress*
- *Practical tips for interpreting daily events*

CHAPTER 6: EXPLORING THE FOUR SUITS

- *Cups, Pentacles, Swords, and Wands explained*
- *Elements, themes, and general meanings*
- *Reading suit combinations in a spread*

CHAPTER 7: WORKING WITH COURT CARDS

- *Pages, Knights, Queens, and Kings in each suit*
- *Personality traits vs. situational energies*
- *Strategies to interpret Court Cards clearly*

CHAPTER 8: CHOOSING THE RIGHT TAROT DECK

- *Art style, theme, and personal resonance*
- *Popular decks and their unique features*
- *Tips for selecting decks that match your style*

CHAPTER 9: CARING FOR YOUR TAROT DECK

- *Storing, cleansing, and bonding with your cards*
- *Physical upkeep to avoid wear and damage*
- *Respectful handling and energetic "reset" methods*

CHAPTER 10: SETTING UP YOUR READING SPACE

- *Environment, mood, and practical setup*
- *Lighting, background music, and privacy*
- *Creating a comfortable atmosphere for focus*

CHAPTER 11: SHUFFLING AND HANDLING TECHNIQUES

- *Overhand, riffle, pile, and wash methods*
- *Letting others shuffle vs. reader-only shuffling*
- *Dealing with reversals and clarifier cards*

CHAPTER 12: SIMPLE AND ADVANCED CARD SPREADS

- *One-card, three-card, and Celtic Cross basics*
- *Designing custom layouts for deeper insight*
- *Tips for matching spreads to specific questions*

CHAPTER 13: READING THE SYMBOLS AND IMAGES

- *Key symbols in Tarot and their meanings*
- *Using color, body language, and setting*
- *Personal and cultural influences on interpretation*

CHAPTER 14: USING INTUITION AND INNER SENSES

- *Balancing logic with gut feeling*
- *Methods to develop and trust intuition*
- *Avoiding over-analysis and nurturing insight*

CHAPTER 15: DOING A READING FOR YOURSELF

- *Objectivity and overcoming personal bias*
- *Choosing spreads for self-reflection*
- *Handling emotional or challenging truths*

CHAPTER 16: DOING A READING FOR OTHERS

- *Respectful communication and question framing*
- *Establishing trust and boundaries*
- *Delivering messages with empathy and clarity*

CHAPTER 17: ETHICS AND RESPONSIBILITY IN TAROT

- *Consent, privacy, and confidentiality*
- *Handling sensitive topics and respecting limits*
- *Fairness, honesty, and protecting yourself and querents*

CHAPTER 18: OVERCOMING READING CHALLENGES

- *Contradictory cards, emotional overload, skepticism*
- *Guiding repeated questions and "scary" cards*
- *Self-care and troubleshooting difficult spreads*

CHAPTER 19: ADVANCED METHODS AND TECHNIQUES

- *Blending Tarot with astrology, numerology, crystals*
- *Layered spreads, rituals, and shadow work*
- *Refined use of reversed cards and specialized readings*

CHAPTER 20: GROWING AS A TAROT READER

- *Tracking progress and celebrating milestones*
- *Exploring new decks, sharing with the community*
- *Maintaining a curious, open, and compassionate approach*

Chapter 1: Introduction to Tarot

1.1 What Is Tarot?

Tarot is a set of 78 cards that people use for personal guidance and self-reflection. Each card has images, symbols, and names that help tell a story. Many people think Tarot is about telling the future, but that is not the full story. While some folks do use Tarot to guess what might happen, a more common approach is to see it as a tool for thinking more clearly about life.

Think of each Tarot card like a page in a storybook. Every page has a picture and a theme. When you look at these pictures, you can learn something about your feelings, your choices, and your plans for the future. Tarot is not magic in the sense of waving a wand. Instead, it is more like a mirror. It lets you look into your own mind and heart, helping you spot hidden thoughts or worries.

People from many different backgrounds enjoy using Tarot. You do not have to be a fortune-teller. You do not have to believe in any particular religion. You only need an open mind and a willingness to learn. Some folks keep a Tarot deck at home to draw a card each morning. Others sit with a friend, shuffle the cards, and see if they can uncover guidance. Whether you are a scientist, an artist, a parent, or a student, you might find that Tarot speaks to you in a unique way.

1.2 Why People Use Tarot

Tarot cards can serve many purposes. Below are some of the reasons people pick up a Tarot deck:

1. **Personal Reflection**: Sometimes you want to understand yourself better. You may ask questions like, "Why do I feel

stuck?" or "What is the right path forward?" Drawing a few Tarot cards can offer new ways of looking at your thoughts.
2. **Problem-Solving**: When faced with difficult choices, it helps to see your situation from a new angle. The images and symbols in Tarot can spark ideas you might not have considered otherwise. A single card might remind you of a memory or a lesson. That reminder can guide you in solving problems.
3. **Emotional Support**: Life can be stressful. Tarot cards, with their gentle advice, can soothe your worries. It is almost like having a trusted friend who listens without judgment. When you pull a card that says, "Things might be tough now, but they will get better," you can find hope.
4. **Spiritual Growth**: Some people see Tarot as part of a spiritual practice. They like to meditate on the cards. They may journal about the meanings of the images. Others light candles or incense to create a calm atmosphere before drawing cards.
5. **Fun and Creativity**: Not every Tarot reading has to be serious. Some people love the art on the cards and enjoy collecting different decks. They might make up stories based on the images. They might draw a spread just for the fun of it. This playfulness can spark creativity.

1.3 Myths and Truths

There are many myths about Tarot. Some believe that Tarot is only used to predict the future in a scary or mysterious way. Others worry that Tarot is bad or evil. Let us clear up these misunderstandings:

- **Myth**: Tarot cards can only be used by special people with "psychic powers."
  Truth: Anyone can learn to read Tarot. You do not need to be a mind-reader or speak with spirits. Learning to read Tarot is

like learning to play a musical instrument. With practice, you get better.
- **Myth**: Tarot always predicts doom.
Truth: Many Tarot cards are positive. Some cards do point to challenges, but they also point to ways to overcome them. Life is made up of good times and bad times. Tarot reflects both.
- **Myth**: You must follow strict rules about how to store, shuffle, or pick your Tarot deck.
Truth: Traditions exist, but they are not set in stone. If you want to wrap your deck in silk, that is fine. If you want to keep it in a plain box, that is also fine. Do what feels right to you and treat your deck with respect.
- **Myth**: Tarot is a magical fix for all problems.
Truth: Tarot is a tool, not a solution machine. It helps guide you. Real changes happen when you take action. If a card suggests improving your communication skills, you still need to put in the effort.

1.4 Basic Structure of the Tarot

A Tarot deck has 78 cards divided into two main parts: the Major Arcana and the Minor Arcana.

1. **Major Arcana (22 cards)**: These are the "big idea" cards. They often deal with major changes or life lessons. For example, The Fool card can suggest a fresh start or a leap of faith. Death can represent transformation and new beginnings, not just physical endings.
2. **Minor Arcana (56 cards)**: These cards talk about everyday life. They are divided into four suits: Cups, Pentacles (also called Coins), Swords, and Wands. Each suit has 14 cards, numbered from Ace to 10, plus four Court Cards (Page, Knight, Queen, and King).

Together, these 78 cards form a complete picture of the human experience. The Major Arcana cards highlight big, life-changing moments. The Minor Arcana cards highlight daily ups and downs.

1.5 How To Approach Tarot as a Beginner

When you first start, you might feel confused. There are many cards, each with different names and images. Do not worry. Like learning a new language, it takes time.

Here are some tips:

1. **Pick a Deck You Like**: There are many types of Tarot decks. Some have very simple artwork. Others are quite detailed. Choose one that catches your eye. You will be more motivated to learn if you enjoy looking at the pictures.
2. **Start With One Card a Day**: Pull one card each morning. Look at it. Notice the colors, the people, the symbols. Ask yourself, "What do I feel when I see this card?" and "How might this relate to my day?" Write down your thoughts.
3. **Keep a Tarot Journal**: It helps to have a notebook or journal. You can write the name of the card, your first impressions, and any situations that come to mind. Over time, you will see patterns.
4. **Use Simple Spreads**: A "spread" is a way of laying out the cards. Beginners often start with a one-card draw or a three-card spread (like Past, Present, Future). These are easy to remember and give enough information without overload.
5. **Be Open**: If a card seems confusing, that is normal. Try to remain curious rather than frustrated. You might look up its meaning in a guidebook or online. But also trust your own intuition. Sometimes your personal feeling about a card is stronger than any text definition.

1.6 The Role of Intuition

Intuition is like a quiet voice inside you that knows things before your mind does. You might notice subtle hints, like a hunch that a friend is sad even though they are smiling. Tarot readings rely on this same sense. When you see a card, you might instantly think of someone you know or a situation you faced. That is your intuition at work.

People sometimes say, "I am not intuitive." But everyone has a degree of intuition. Think about times you sensed something was off without being told. Think about when you just "knew" which choice to make. By practicing Tarot, you build a stronger connection with this part of yourself.

1.7 Common Uses of Tarot

Daily Guidance: You can pull a card in the morning to get an idea of what energy or theme might appear in your day. It might not always match exactly what happens, but it can give you something to reflect on.

Decision Making: If you face a tough choice, you can ask the Tarot, "What do I need to know about taking this job?" or "How can I handle this conflict with a friend?" The cards can point out pros, cons, or hidden elements.

Personal Growth: Some people use Tarot cards to understand their personal growth. They might do monthly or yearly readings to see patterns or goals. They can compare cards they draw over time to spot improvements.

Storytelling and Creativity: Writers and artists sometimes use Tarot to break creative blocks. They draw cards to develop plots or characters. They might ask, "What does my main character need to learn?" and then see what card shows up.

1.8 Sample Insights From a Tarot Reading

Imagine you ask, "How can I improve my communication skills?" and you draw the Three of Cups. This card often shows three people celebrating or toasting. It is about friendships, gatherings, and good times. From this, you might guess that being more open and friendly could help. Or you might realize you should spend more time around the people you care about. The idea of coming together with others is key.

On the other hand, if you draw the Five of Swords, which might show a person holding swords while others walk away, this could indicate conflict or misunderstandings. It suggests that you need to be careful about how you speak. You might want to avoid being too harsh or argumentative.

Tarot does not force you to do anything, but it can highlight patterns in your relationships or your thoughts. By reflecting on these insights, you can make better choices.

1.9 Is Tarot a Fortune-Telling Tool or a Mirror?

A big question is whether Tarot really predicts the future. The answer often depends on the reader's belief. Some people do believe the cards have mystical powers that can show events yet to happen. Others see Tarot as more of a mirror, reflecting your current mindset and possible outcomes if you do not change anything.

In many cases, it is best to see Tarot as a tool for guidance. It can highlight potential outcomes based on your current path. But we all have free will. If a card suggests a struggle is coming, you can take steps to avoid or reduce that struggle. If the reading points to positive opportunities, you can work to make them happen faster.

1.10 Handling Misinterpretations

If you are a beginner, it is easy to feel worried if you draw a card like The Tower or Death. These cards look dramatic. The Tower might show a tall building on fire. Death might show a skeleton or a grim figure. However, these cards can mean transformation, sudden changes, or the end of a difficult situation. The key is to read carefully. Look beyond the scary image.

Here is a tip: try not to jump to conclusions. Take a deep breath. Read the card's meaning in a reliable guide, and use your intuition to see how it might apply to your situation. Over time, you will grow more comfortable.

1.11 Respecting the Tarot

Many readers see Tarot as something special and deserving of respect. This respect includes:

- Storing your deck in a clean, dry place.
- Handling the cards gently.
- Not using the cards in ways that feel wrong or dishonest.

This does not mean you must follow rigid rules. It just means treating the cards the way you would treat a valued tool or a beloved book.

1.12 Ethical Considerations

While we will talk more about ethics in a later chapter, it is worth mentioning here that Tarot readers have a responsibility. You might read cards for yourself or for friends. Either way, you want to be honest about what the cards are saying. Avoid making scary or harmful claims. If someone comes to you for a reading and shares personal struggles, respect their privacy. Make it clear that Tarot does not replace professional help in areas like health or law.

1.13 Choosing Questions to Ask

When you read Tarot, the question matters. Vague questions can lead to vague answers. Here are some examples of good and less-helpful questions:

- **Less Helpful**: "Will I be happy?"
  This question is too broad. The cards might not give a clear picture.
- **Better**: "What steps can I take to feel happier?"
  This focuses on what you can do. It is action-based and invites guidance.
- **Less Helpful**: "Will I get married next year?"
  This question can trap you into a yes/no mindset.
- **Better**: "What do I need to know about building a healthy relationship?"
  This opens the door to more in-depth advice about love and companionship.

1.14 Common Fears

- **Fear of Negative Cards**: People worry about getting "bad" cards. But remember, all cards have lessons to offer. A card that seems negative can warn you or help you grow.
- **Fear of Doing It Wrong**: Beginners might think they have to memorize all meanings perfectly. Tarot is an art, not a strict set of rules. Two readers might look at the same card and see different angles. That is normal.
- **Fear of Judgment**: Some folks worry about being judged by friends or family who think Tarot is strange. Often, once

people understand Tarot is a reflection tool and not about scary rituals, they become more accepting.

1.15 Simple Reading Example

Let us say you do a three-card spread asking about a new job. The positions are **Past**, **Present**, and **Future**. You draw:

1. **Past**: The Hermit
2. **Present**: Two of Pentacles
3. **Future**: Ace of Wands
- **Hermit (Past)**: This suggests a time of introspection or isolation. Maybe you spent a lot of time studying or thinking about your life direction in the past.
- **Two of Pentacles (Present)**: This card often shows a person juggling two coins. It can mean you are trying to balance multiple responsibilities or choices.
- **Ace of Wands (Future)**: Aces often suggest new beginnings, and Wands can mean creativity or passion. This might hint that a new job or project could spark energy and excitement soon.

Putting it all together, the reading might say: "You have thought long and hard about what job to pursue (Hermit). You are now juggling your options (Two of Pentacles). Soon, you might have a fresh start that energizes you (Ace of Wands)." This does not mean you absolutely will get a job. But it does point to good energy and possibility.

1.16 Practical Tips for Beginners

- **Practice Regularly**: The more you read, the easier it gets.
- **Study the Images**: Notice colors, facial expressions, and scenery. Each detail can add meaning.

- **Use Your Own Words**: When you explain a card, do not just memorize definitions. Try describing the picture in your own way.
- **Stay Patient**: Tarot is a journey. It is normal to feel overwhelmed at first.
- **Ask for Feedback**: If you read for friends, ask them if your interpretation makes sense. Feedback helps you learn.

1.17 Different Tarot Decks

The most popular deck is the Rider-Waite-Smith deck (often just called the Rider-Waite deck). This deck has been around since 1909. It is known for its bright colors and clear pictures. Many books and lessons are based on this deck. However, there are others like the Thoth Tarot and the Marseille Tarot. Each deck has its style and symbolism. You might start with a classic deck, then explore more themes later.

1.18 Using Tarot in Daily Life

Tarot does not have to be a formal event. You can integrate it into your daily routine:

- **Morning Draw**: Pull a card to see what energy might define your day.
- **Bedtime Reflection**: Pull a card and ask, "What should I learn from today?"
- **Creative Break**: When stuck, shuffle the cards and see if the imagery sparks new ideas.
- **Goal Setting**: Draw a card to explore what might help you reach a goal.

1.19 Common Missteps to Avoid

- **Forgetting Context**: If you pull a card about a relationship, do not forget the other factors. For instance, if you see a card suggesting conflict, ask yourself if you are already arguing with your partner. The reading might highlight something that is already happening, not something brand new.
- **Treating Tarot as a Crutch**: Relying on Tarot for every tiny decision can become too much. It is fine to seek guidance, but do not forget your common sense and personal wisdom.
- **Refusing to Learn**: If you keep seeing a particular card but do not bother to learn its meaning, you might miss out on helpful insights. A little study can go a long way.

1.20 Wrapping Up Chapter 1

We have covered the basics of Tarot: what it is, why people use it, and how to start. Remember, Tarot is a friendly companion on your life journey. It can help you think in new ways, ask new questions, and maybe even spot solutions you did not see before. As you begin, keep an open mind, be patient, and enjoy the process. In the next chapter, we will dig into the history of Tarot and see how these cards traveled from simple beginnings to their widespread use today.

Chapter 2: A Brief History of Tarot

2.1 Early Origins of Playing Cards

To understand the history of Tarot, we need to look at the roots of playing cards in general. Playing cards are believed to have originated in China, where paper was invented. Over time, these cards traveled west through trade routes, eventually reaching Europe. In the beginning, playing cards were mostly used for games and gambling. They were not seen as mystical tools.

Historians often mention that by the late 14th century, playing cards started appearing in Europe. They were hand-painted and quite expensive. Only wealthy families could afford them. Over the years, printing methods improved, making cards cheaper and more common.

2.2 Birth of Tarot in Europe

Tarot, as we know it, likely began in northern Italy in the 15th century. It started as a card game called "Tarocchi." At first, these Tarot cards were used like regular playing cards. People played trick-taking games, similar to how some might play Bridge today. The earliest Tarot decks we know about were expensive, hand-painted works of art, created for nobles.

These early Tarot decks had four suits, much like standard playing cards. But they also included a series of special picture cards we now call the Major Arcana. These special cards depicted characters like The Emperor, The Empress, and The Pope (or The Hierophant, in modern decks). They added excitement and complexity to the card game.

2.3 The Major Arcana as "Triumphs"

In medieval Italy, these extra cards in the Tarot deck were sometimes called "trionfi," which means "triumphs." They were like extra trump cards. The word "trump" in card games comes from the idea of "triumph." These special cards could beat the regular suits. People enjoyed this style of play, and the Tarot deck spread to different parts of Europe.

During this time, no one was using Tarot cards to tell fortunes in any official capacity. They were simply part of a popular card game among certain circles. Yet, the elaborate images of the Major Arcana likely made people think about deeper meanings. Symbols like The Wheel of Fortune or Judgment pointed to moral or religious ideas of the time.

2.4 Changes in France

Tarot became popular in France, where it was called "Tarot" (pronounced differently in French). It continued to be mainly a game. However, over time, something interesting happened. People began to connect these cards with mystical ideas and hidden knowledge. By the 18th century, some French writers and occult scholars started linking Tarot to ancient Egypt, the Kabbalah (a form of Jewish mysticism), and other secret traditions. While these connections were not proven historically, they captured people's imaginations.

2.5 The Occult Revival

In the late 18th and 19th centuries, Europe experienced a wave of interest in secret societies, magic, and esoteric teachings. Groups like the Freemasons and the Rosicrucians intrigued intellectuals with their hidden rituals. Occultists, or people who studied hidden knowledge, looked at Tarot cards and saw more than just a game. They believed the images held codes related to ancient wisdom.

People like Antoine Court de Gébelin claimed that Tarot symbolism came from ancient Egyptian texts. Although scholars today say there is no solid evidence for that, the idea was very popular back then. Other writers expanded on these theories, adding layers of mystical meaning to each Tarot card.

2.6 Etteilla and the Rise of Fortune Telling

One of the earliest known figures to popularize Tarot as a tool for fortune telling was Jean-Baptiste Alliette, who went by the pen name "Etteilla" (his last name spelled backward). In the 1780s, Etteilla wrote books on how to use Tarot for divination. He created his own deck, rearranging the cards and adding instructions for reading them.

Etteilla taught that each card had a specific meaning for predicting events and personalities. This was quite different from the original card game. But it caught on among those who were curious about the occult. As more people read Etteilla's books, Tarot's reputation as a fortune-telling device grew.

2.7 The 19th Century: Further Growth

Throughout the 19th century, various secret groups and scholars kept adding new interpretations to Tarot. They linked it to astrology, numerology, and alchemy. Writers published manuals describing how each card aligned with certain planets, zodiac signs, or letters of the Hebrew alphabet. This made the Tarot deck seem like a coded map of the universe.

At the same time, Tarot card games continued. In places like France, Italy, and Switzerland, people still played Tarot just for fun. So we had two different groups using the same deck: some were playing a traditional card game, and others were using the cards to explore spiritual and mystical ideas.

2.8 The British Influence: The Hermetic Order of the Golden Dawn

Toward the end of the 19th century, a British secret society called the Hermetic Order of the Golden Dawn became famous. Many important figures in the occult world were members. They wrote complicated teachings about magic, the Kabbalah, and Tarot. They saw the Tarot as a key to understanding the mysteries of life. Each card was linked to paths on the Kabbalistic Tree of Life, as well as to certain colors, astrological signs, and more.

One of the Golden Dawn members was Arthur Edward Waite. He partnered with artist Pamela Colman Smith to create one of the most famous Tarot decks in history: the Rider-Waite-Smith deck (often just called the Rider-Waite deck). First published in 1909, this deck became widely used and studied, especially in English-speaking countries.

2.9 The Creation of the Rider-Waite-Smith Deck

Arthur Edward Waite wanted a deck that reflected his understanding of mysticism. Pamela Colman Smith provided the artwork, which included rich imagery for each of the 78 cards. Unlike many older Tarot decks, the Minor Arcana cards in the Rider-Waite-Smith deck showed full scenes rather than just symbols or suit icons. For instance, the Five of Pentacles depicted two poor figures walking in the snow near a church window. This was a big shift. It helped readers memorize and intuitively sense the meaning of each card.

The deck was published by the Rider Company, and because of that, it earned the name "Rider-Waite." Over time, people noticed Pamela Colman Smith's contribution and started adding her name, calling it the "Rider-Waite-Smith deck." This deck introduced many people to Tarot. It remains the basis for countless modern decks and reference books.

2.10 Other Important Figures and Decks

Alongside Waite and Smith, there were other figures who shaped modern Tarot:

- **Aleister Crowley**: A member of the Golden Dawn who later created the Thoth Tarot deck with artist Lady Frieda Harris. This deck also used vivid, symbolic art and included Crowley's unique ideas about magic and spirituality.
- **Paul Foster Case**: An American occultist who founded the Builders of the Adytum (B.O.T.A.). He created a Tarot deck with a strong focus on the relationship between Tarot, the Kabbalah, and color symbolism.
- **Joseph Campbell**: Though not directly a Tarot creator, Campbell's work on myths and the "hero's journey" influenced how some read and interpret Tarot, especially the Major Arcana as stages of personal growth.

2.11 Tarot in the 20th Century

As the 20th century progressed, Tarot spread throughout the world. Newspapers and magazines sometimes featured "Tarot columns" similar to horoscope columns. You could find small booklets in bookstores about reading Tarot. The New Age movement of the 1960s and 1970s also boosted interest in all forms of divination, including Tarot.

By the 1980s and 1990s, more people were treating Tarot not just as a way to tell fortunes, but as a tool for personal development and psychological insight. Writers like Mary K. Greer and Rachel Pollack published books that explored the deeper meanings of the cards. They connected Tarot with Jungian psychology, seeing the archetypes of the Major Arcana as reflections of the human psyche.

2.12 Tarot in Popular Culture

Over time, Tarot made its way into movies, TV shows, and novels. You might see a fortune-teller character in a film using Tarot cards to warn the hero of danger or reveal a hidden secret. While these portrayals can be dramatic or spooky, they also introduced more people to the concept of Tarot.

In some cases, Tarot imagery showed up in music album covers, fashion designs, and even video games. The mysterious look of the cards fit well with creative storytelling. However, this also led to more confusion or stereotypes. Some folks thought of Tarot only as a prop for scary scenes. But the truth is, Tarot can be as calm and helpful as any self-help tool.

2.13 The Modern Tarot Renaissance

In the late 20th and early 21st century, there has been a surge in the creation of new Tarot decks. Artists across the globe have taken the basic template of 78 cards and infused it with their cultural background, personal style, or thematic interests. You can find decks that focus on animals, fantasy worlds, African myths, pop culture, feminism, and much more.

The internet allowed Tarot enthusiasts to form communities, share readings, and learn from each other. Websites, online courses, and social media groups made it easier than ever for beginners to dive in. You no longer had to hide your interest for fear of judgment.

Many people now see Tarot as a form of art or a self-improvement tool. It is not just for "fortune tellers."

2.14 Debunking the Egypt Connection

A large part of Tarot's mystical reputation came from the idea that it was derived from the Book of Thoth in ancient Egypt. While this story adds a romantic flair, most historians agree there is no solid evidence that Tarot came from Egyptian temples. It is true that Aleister Crowley named his deck the "Thoth Tarot," but that was based on his own beliefs, not on a proven link to ancient Egyptian religion.

Still, the myth persisted for centuries. Why? Likely because ancient Egypt was considered a place of deep, hidden wisdom. Many 18th and 19th-century thinkers found it appealing to connect Tarot's rich images with the grandeur of Egyptian culture. While fun to consider, this story remains a legend rather than a historical fact.

2.15 Tarot's Place in Different Cultures

As Tarot spread worldwide, different cultures adopted it in unique ways. For instance, in Latin America, some readers combine Tarot with local spiritual practices. In parts of Asia, Tarot is sometimes used alongside other fortune-telling methods like palmistry or the I Ching. In these settings, Tarot becomes part of a larger system of understanding life and destiny.

In modern Western countries, Tarot is often seen as part of the New Age or holistic health scene. You can find Tarot readers at fairs, wellness centers, and online. Some people read Tarot as a full-time job, offering personal consultations to clients. Others do it casually for friends and family.

2.16 Skepticism and Tarot

Throughout history, many skeptics have criticized Tarot. They argue that the messages are too vague or that readers use cold reading techniques. Cold reading refers to making general statements that could apply to anyone, then acting as if you are reading a person's mind. While it is true that some unethical people might misuse Tarot, many honest Tarot readers emphasize that the cards are there to encourage reflection, not to declare absolute truths.

As interest in psychology grew, some saw Tarot as a creative way to talk about personal issues. Even skeptics who do not believe in any mystical power might see the value in using Tarot cards to spark a conversation about someone's feelings or goals.

2.17 Tarot Today: A Tool for Self-Discovery

What started as a card game in Italy has now become a global phenomenon with many layers. Some folks still play Tarot card games, especially in parts of Europe. But a great number of people around the world use Tarot for personal insight, meditation, counseling, and more.

Today, you can find Tarot decks in many styles. The Rider-Waite-Smith deck remains the most famous and is often recommended to beginners. The Thoth Tarot deck appeals to those who like Aleister Crowley's approach. There are also decks that follow the Marseille tradition, which is older and has simpler art. Modern artists create decks that blend in their own themes, such as LGBTQ+ awareness, environmentalism, or cultural stories.

2.18 Continuing Evolution

Tarot continues to evolve. People experiment with new spreads, new ways of interpreting old symbols, and new technologies (like Tarot apps on smartphones). Some Tarot enthusiasts do group readings through video calls, sharing the images on screen. Others create online journals and blogs about their daily draws.

In many ways, Tarot acts like a living language. Each generation and community can add to the conversation. That is why you might see huge differences between one Tarot deck and another. But the heart of Tarot remains the same: 78 cards, each with unique images, that can help us see life in a new light.

2.19 Why Learn the History?

You might ask, "Why does the history matter if I just want to learn how to read the cards?" Knowing the history offers a few benefits:

1. **Deeper Appreciation**: Understanding Tarot's roots helps you see how these cards developed and changed. You can sense the richness in each image, knowing that people for centuries found meaning in them.
2. **Respect for Traditions**: You learn about the cultural backgrounds that shaped Tarot. This can add depth to your readings. It also helps you see why some people treat Tarot with respect and even reverence.
3. **Separating Myth from Fact**: By learning the real origins, you avoid false stories that might confuse you. You can still enjoy the legends if they spark your imagination, but you will know the difference between history and fantasy.
4. **Finding Your Path**: Once you know the many ways Tarot has been used—game, fortune-telling device, spiritual guide—you can pick what feels right for you. Maybe you will read the cards in a more psychological way, or maybe you will follow a traditional occult system. The choice is yours.

Chapter 3: Understanding the Tarot Deck

3.1 Overview of the Deck

A Tarot deck has 78 cards. These cards are split into two main groups: the Major Arcana and the Minor Arcana. The **Major Arcana** has 22 cards. These cards deal with big life themes and important changes. The **Minor Arcana** has 56 cards. These cards talk more about day-to-day events and concerns. Each card has its own image, name, and number (except some Court Cards, which have titles instead of numbers).

Tarot cards use symbols to represent ideas and energies. For example, a card might have a sun in the background to show hope or a dove to represent peace. Even the colors can carry meaning. A bright color like yellow might suggest optimism, while gray might suggest doubt. When you learn to read Tarot, you learn to notice these symbols and see how they connect to your own life situation or question.

3.2 The Major Arcana

The Major Arcana consists of 22 cards that often stand for major life lessons. People sometimes call them "trump cards." In a reading, Major Arcana cards tend to stand out, and they might suggest big issues or turning points. These 22 cards start with The Fool (numbered 0) and end with The World (numbered 21). In between, each card represents a step in a journey, often called "The Fool's Journey." We will explore the Major Arcana in detail in Chapter 4, so stay tuned.

Here are some examples of Major Arcana cards:

- **The Fool (0)**: A card of new beginnings.
- **The Magician (1)**: A card of power and skill.
- **Death (13)**: A card of transformation, not always physical death.
- **The World (21)**: A card of completion and fulfillment.

Because the Major Arcana highlights significant energies and turning points, many Tarot readers pay special attention to these cards in a reading. They may suggest the big "themes" in a person's life at the moment.

3.3 The Minor Arcana

The Minor Arcana has 56 cards. These are often more about everyday situations, challenges, or joys. Within the Minor Arcana, there are four suits:

1. **Cups**
2. **Pentacles** (or Coins)
3. **Swords**
4. **Wands**

Each suit contains 14 cards:

- **Ace** through **10** (ten numbered cards)
- **Court Cards**: Page, Knight, Queen, and King

The suits are somewhat like the suits in regular playing cards (like hearts or spades), but Tarot suits have unique themes tied to them. For example, Cups often relate to emotions, while Swords relate to thoughts. We will look at each suit more closely in later chapters.

3.3.1 Ace Through 10

For each suit, cards from Ace to 10 often describe daily events or situations. For instance, an Ace can indicate a fresh start. A 10 might show a sense of completion. Each number in between represents a different step in life's smaller stories.

3.3.2 Court Cards

In each suit, there are four Court Cards: Page, Knight, Queen, and King. Sometimes these are called Princess, Prince, Queen, and King, depending on the deck. These cards might represent people, personality traits, or energies in your life. For example, a Knight could represent someone who is brave but a bit impatient. A Queen might suggest a person who is nurturing or strong in leadership.

3.4 Symbols in the Four Suits

Each of the four suits also carries its own "element" and general theme. These elements help you remember the kind of energy each suit brings to a reading:

1. **Cups**: Connected to the element of **Water**. Often tied to emotions, relationships, and intuition.
2. **Pentacles**: Connected to the element of **Earth**. Often tied to money, career, home life, and material matters.
3. **Swords**: Connected to the element of **Air**. Often tied to thoughts, intellect, conflict, and communication.
4. **Wands**: Connected to the element of **Fire**. Often tied to creativity, ambition, passion, and motivation.

By learning these elemental associations, you can see how a card's suit might hint at what area of life it refers to. If you see many Cup cards in a reading, it might suggest emotional topics. If you see many Sword cards, you might need to pay attention to conflicts or mental challenges.

3.5 Suits vs. Major Arcana

The Major Arcana can be seen as the "big story," while the Minor Arcana is like the "everyday story." When you do a reading, if you see a lot of Major Arcana cards, it might mean something important is happening in your life—like a new relationship, moving to a new city, or a big personal transformation. If you mostly see Minor Arcana cards, the reading might be about smaller, more regular parts of life, like dealing with a coworker or deciding how to budget your money.

However, do not think the Minor Arcana is unimportant. Sometimes, a single Minor Arcana card can have a strong impact on your daily choices. The difference is often about scope: Major Arcana speaks loudly about major life changes, while the Minor Arcana speaks about how those changes might play out day by day.

3.6 Understanding Tarot Imagery

Tarot cards often show people, animals, landscapes, and objects. Each of these images has meaning. For instance, a card might show a person blindfolded. This image can suggest not seeing a situation clearly or feeling stuck. Another card might show a lion, symbolizing courage or power. Certain decks even include angels, fairies, or mythological creatures to add more layers of meaning.

Because there are so many decks out there, the artwork and imagery vary. One deck might have modern cartoon drawings, while another uses Renaissance-style paintings. Despite these differences, the core ideas remain similar because the cards follow the same general structure. As a reader, you will learn to pick up on the images that speak to you. You can ask yourself questions like:

- "Why does this card show water?"
- "What does it mean that the sky is stormy?"
- "Who is the person in this picture looking at?"

By exploring these details, you form a personal bond with each card.

3.7 Different Types of Tarot Decks

While the **Rider-Waite-Smith** deck is the most popular, many other decks exist. Some decks follow the **Thoth** tradition, inspired by Aleister Crowley's teachings. Others follow the **Marseille** style, which has simpler art. Modern decks might have themes like animals, fantasy worlds, cultural art, or even popular movies. When you buy a deck, it usually comes with a "little white book" (LWB) or a guidebook explaining the creator's intended meanings for each card.

3.7.1 Rider-Waite-Smith Deck

- Created in 1909 by Arthur Edward Waite and artist Pamela Colman Smith.
- Features detailed scenes for every card, including all the Minor Arcana.
- Widely used, making it easy to find resources and guides for learning.

3.7.2 Thoth Deck

- Created by Aleister Crowley and painted by Lady Frieda Harris.
- Uses rich symbols, geometry, and sometimes different names for certain cards (e.g., "Adjustment" instead of "Justice").
- Emphasizes magical and esoteric ideas.

3.7.3 Marseille Deck

- One of the oldest styles, coming from regions of France and Switzerland.
- Simplified images, especially in the Minor Arcana (many show repeated suit symbols instead of detailed scenes).
- Traditional look appealing to historians and classic Tarot players.

3.7.4 Themed Decks

- These can feature anything from dragons to cats, from steampunk art to fairy tales.
- The core 78-card structure remains, but the images are adapted to the theme.
- Great for collectors or those who resonate with a particular motif.

3.8 Choosing Your Deck

Picking a deck can be fun. Some people say a deck has to be "given" to you as a gift, but that is more of an old tale than a rule. You can buy your own deck if you want. Look for artwork that speaks to you. Flip through a sample if possible. You want a deck you feel comfortable with. When you like the pictures, you might find it easier to remember the meanings.

People sometimes ask, "Can I have more than one deck?" Absolutely. Over time, you might collect different decks for different purposes. Maybe you use one deck for personal readings and another deck for readings with friends. Some readers even switch decks depending on the question. There are no strict rules—just choose what feels right for you.

3.9 Storing and Cleansing Your Deck

Because Tarot decks are special tools, many readers like to store them carefully. You can keep them in the box they came in or use a pouch or bag. Some people wrap their cards in a cloth. Others place them in a wooden box. The idea is to protect the cards from damage and keep them together.

Some readers also "cleanse" their deck to clear any stagnant energy. This could mean:

- Leaving the deck in moonlight overnight.
- Smudging the deck with incense.
- Knocking on the deck three times to reset its energy.
- Placing a crystal on top of the deck.

These practices are optional, but they can help you feel more connected to the cards. It is like having a little ritual that says, "These cards are fresh and ready to guide me."

3.10 Bonding With the Cards

Many experienced readers suggest spending time with each card. You can flip through the deck, look at each image, and note your initial feelings. Ask yourself, "What is going on in this picture?" or "How would I feel if I were inside this scene?" You can also journal about the card, describing the symbols and how they might apply to your life.

Some people do a "card-a-day" exercise. Each morning, they draw a single card and reflect on its meaning. They might also check back at night to see if that card related to the day's events. Over time, this practice helps you memorize the cards and develop your own interpretation style.

3.11 Anatomy of a Tarot Card

Although every Tarot deck is different, most cards share some common elements:

- **Title/Number**: Major Arcana cards have a name (like "Temperance") and a number (like 14). Minor Arcana cards are identified by their suit and number (like "5 of Wands") or by their role if they are Court Cards (like "Queen of Cups").
- **Central Image**: Each card usually has one main image or scene. It might be a person, a group of people, an animal, or a symbolic object.
- **Background/Setting**: The background can include skies, buildings, mountains, or water. These details can add extra layers of meaning.
- **Colors**: Artists choose certain colors to reflect the card's mood. Bright colors might suggest joy, while darker colors might hint at challenges or sorrow.

By paying attention to all these pieces, you get a well-rounded understanding of each card.

3.12 Reverse Cards

Some readers use reversed cards. This means if you shuffle and a card appears upside down, you read it as a "reversal." A reversed card can mean an opposite or a delayed energy. For example, if **The Sun** is about joy, it might mean you are not feeling that joy as strongly when reversed. Or if the **Two of Cups** is about partnership, reversed might suggest miscommunication.

Other readers choose not to read reversed cards at all. They keep every card upright. Instead, they rely on intuition and the context of the reading to decide if a meaning is positive, challenging, delayed, or blocked. Whether you use reversals is a personal choice. There is no right or wrong way.

3.13 Making Sense of Card Combinations

A single card can tell you something, but when you put multiple cards together in a spread, the meanings can evolve. For example, drawing the **Eight of Pentacles** (hard work and skill) and the **Chariot** (motivation and victory) might suggest your career is about to take off due to your dedication. However, drawing the **Eight of Pentacles** next to the **Nine of Swords** (worry and anxiety) might hint you are overworking yourself, leading to stress.

Learning to combine the meanings of multiple cards is a skill that grows with practice. Each card can affect the interpretation of the others, creating a story rather than just a set of separate messages.

3.14 Common Confusions

3.14.1 Major Arcana vs. Minor Arcana

Beginners can get confused about why we separate them. Remember that Major Arcana cards usually refer to big life lessons, while Minor Arcana cards talk about daily, everyday themes. If you see a reading with many Major Arcana cards, it might mean a life-changing period is unfolding.

3.14.2 Court Cards

Court Cards can be tricky because they may represent either:

- A specific person in your life.
- A side of your own personality.
- An energy or approach you need to adopt.

You have to decide which interpretation fits the reading. If you are reading about your workplace and you pull the Knight of Wands, it might represent a coworker who is very driven or impulsive. Or it could mean you need to be bold and adventurous like a Knight of Wands in your job.

3.14.3 Suits vs. Elements

A beginner might confuse suits with their matching elements. A quick reminder:

- **Cups = Water** (emotions, relationships)
- **Pentacles = Earth** (money, home, physical needs)
- **Swords = Air** (thoughts, communication)
- **Wands = Fire** (creativity, action)

3.15 Developing Your Personal Reading Style

Over time, you will notice certain suits or cards show up a lot in your readings. You might form a special relationship with them. For instance, maybe the **Queen of Cups** appears whenever you need self-care. Or the **Ace of Swords** keeps popping up when you have a new idea. These personal patterns are part of developing your style as a Tarot reader.

Some people use traditional definitions from books. Others rely on the images and their intuition. Many do both. You might start by reading the "little white book" that came with your deck, then over time, add your own insights. The great thing about Tarot is that it can be both structured (with known meanings) and fluid (with personal impressions).

3.16 Questions and Card Meanings

When you do a reading, your question can shape how you see a card. For example, if your question is about love, and you draw the **Three of Pentacles**, you might interpret it as cooperation and teamwork in a relationship. If your question is about your job, the same **Three of Pentacles** might suggest working well with colleagues or joining a new project team.

Context matters. The same card can point to different things depending on the question or the spread.

3.17 Becoming Familiar with the Deck

One of the best ways to truly understand your Tarot deck is to spend time with it. Here are some simple exercises:

1. **Daily Draw**: Pull a card each morning or evening. Write down or think about what it might mean for your day.
2. **Compare Suits**: Pick one suit—say, Cups—and lay out all 14 cards in numerical order. Notice how the story seems to move from the Ace to the 10, and how the Court Cards differ.
3. **Practice Readings**: Do small readings for yourself or a friend. Pay attention to how the cards work together.
4. **Card Storytelling**: Pick three random cards and weave a short story that connects them. This helps you see how they interact.

3.18 Avoiding Overwhelm

With 78 cards, it is easy to feel overwhelmed. Remember, you do not have to memorize everything at once. Focus on a few cards a week. Let yourself get to know their names and images. Over time, you will have a good sense of all 78 cards. It might take months or even years to feel fully confident, and that is okay. Tarot is a journey, not a race.

3.19 FAQs

Q: Do I need to learn the astrological or numerological meanings of each card?
A: You do not have to. Some readers love to dive into astrology and numerology. Others prefer to keep it simple. You can explore these topics if they interest you, but it is not required to do a good reading.

Q: Is it okay to use Tarot just for fun?
A: Of course! Some people use Tarot as a way to spark creativity or break the ice at gatherings. As long as you respect the cards and the people involved, you can enjoy Tarot in a playful way.

Q: What if I draw a "bad" card?
A: There are no truly "bad" cards. Some, like The Tower or the 10 of Swords, look scary. But they can also mean breakthroughs, endings that lead to better beginnings, or necessary change. Try to see the message in every card.

Chapter 4: The Major Arcana Cards

4.1 Introduction to the Major Arcana

The Major Arcana is often called the "heart" of the Tarot deck. It has 22 cards, numbered from 0 to 21. Each card has a unique name and image, and each one symbolizes an important stage or theme in life. Many Tarot teachers say these 22 cards tell the story of "The Fool's Journey," which is a symbolic path from innocence (Card 0: The Fool) to completeness (Card 21: The World).

When you do a Tarot reading, Major Arcana cards often stand out because they point to bigger lessons. You might think of them as signposts along the road of life. If several Major Arcana cards appear, it can suggest that you are dealing with strong or long-lasting influences. Each card can also carry both positive and challenging qualities, so it is helpful to look at the imagery, the number, and the name to find the message that fits your situation.

Below, we will explore each Major Arcana card in order. We will give a simple explanation of its general meaning and possible advice for real-life situations.

4.2 The Fool (0)

- **Imagery**: Often shows a young person on a journey, sometimes about to step off a cliff.
- **Theme**: New beginnings, optimism, a leap of faith.

- **Meaning**: The Fool suggests you might be starting a new chapter or taking a risk. It encourages you to have faith and embrace the unknown with an open heart. However, it also advises caution so you do not rush without thinking.
- **Advice**: Be brave and stay open-minded. Trust that every journey begins with a single step.

4.3 The Magician (1)

- **Imagery**: A figure with one arm raised, often with symbols of the four suits (Cup, Pentacle, Sword, Wand) on a table.
- **Theme**: Power, skill, manifestation.
- **Meaning**: The Magician represents the power to create, focusing your will to make things happen. If this card appears, it suggests you have the tools and skills you need to achieve your goal.
- **Advice**: Take action. Use your talents wisely. Believe that you can shape your situation through your efforts.

4.4 The High Priestess (2)

- **Imagery**: A mysterious woman seated between two pillars, named Boaz and Jachin in some decks.
- **Theme**: Intuition, secrets, hidden knowledge.
- **Meaning**: The High Priestess points to the importance of your inner voice. It can also mean there is something beneath the surface that you have yet to discover.
- **Advice**: Listen closely to your gut feelings. Let quiet reflection guide you before making decisions.

4.5 The Empress (3)

- **Imagery**: A regal woman often surrounded by nature or holding a shield with a Venus symbol.
- **Theme**: Fertility, abundance, creativity.
- **Meaning**: The Empress stands for motherly care and growth, whether in literal parenthood or creative projects. She can also signal comfort and a time of prosperity.
- **Advice**: Nurture yourself and your ideas. Show kindness and watch good things blossom in return.

4.6 The Emperor (4)

- **Imagery**: A stern figure on a throne, often associated with the ram (Aries).
- **Theme**: Authority, structure, leadership.
- **Meaning**: The Emperor represents discipline, rules, and a stable foundation. If this card appears, it might be time to organize your life or step into a leadership role.
- **Advice**: Take charge of your situation. Use logic and structure to bring order where needed.

4.7 The Hierophant (5)

- **Imagery**: A spiritual figure, sometimes called The Pope, with followers at his feet.
- **Theme**: Tradition, belief systems, guidance.

- **Meaning**: The Hierophant highlights lessons from tradition or mentors. It can point to formal education, religious practice, or other structured beliefs.
- **Advice**: Respect traditions that offer wisdom, but also be aware if they limit your growth. Seek guidance from trusted sources.

4.8 The Lovers (6)

- **Imagery**: Two figures (often Adam and Eve in some decks), with an angel overseeing them.
- **Theme**: Love, choices, relationships.
- **Meaning**: The Lovers can indicate romance or the need to make an important choice, often about values or commitments. It may speak to unity but also the responsibility that comes with it.
- **Advice**: If faced with a big decision, choose with your heart and be true to your beliefs. In relationships, seek balance and mutual respect.

4.9 The Chariot (7)

- **Imagery**: A figure in a chariot, sometimes pulled by two sphinxes or horses of opposite colors.
- **Theme**: Determination, victory, control.
- **Meaning**: The Chariot represents forward momentum and overcoming obstacles. It can suggest travel, ambition, and the drive to succeed.
- **Advice**: Stay focused. Harness any conflicting forces (like doubts or distractions) and steer them toward your goal.

4.10 Strength (8)

- **Imagery**: A woman gently taming a lion.
- **Theme**: Inner strength, compassion, courage.
- **Meaning**: This card emphasizes quiet power that comes from patience and compassion, rather than force.
- **Advice**: Approach challenges with calm confidence. Sometimes kindness wins where aggression fails.

4.11 The Hermit (9)

- **Imagery**: An old man holding a lantern, often standing on a mountain.
- **Theme**: Soul-searching, solitude, wisdom.
- **Meaning**: The Hermit suggests taking time away from the noise of daily life to reflect and find inner guidance. It can also mean seeking a teacher or mentor.
- **Advice**: Give yourself space to think. Quiet reflection can lead to answers you will not find in a crowd.

4.12 The Wheel of Fortune (10)

- **Imagery**: A large wheel with various creatures around it, sometimes including the letters T-O-R-A or T-A-R-O.
- **Theme**: Change, cycles, fate.

- **Meaning**: The Wheel of Fortune reminds us that life moves in cycles. Good times follow bad times, and vice versa. It can indicate a turning point or unexpected event.
- **Advice**: Be flexible and open to change. If fortune turns in your favor, ride the wave. If not, remember it will eventually shift again.

4.13 Justice (11)

- **Imagery**: A figure with scales in one hand and a sword in the other, often sitting between two pillars.
- **Theme**: Fairness, truth, balance.
- **Meaning**: Justice speaks of cause and effect, responsibility, and making decisions with honesty. In some decks, Justice is numbered 8 while Strength is 11, but the meaning remains similar.
- **Advice**: Consider all sides of an issue before acting. Seek fairness and clarity in your choices.

4.14 The Hanged Man (12)

- **Imagery**: A person hanging upside down from a tree, looking calm rather than upset.
- **Theme**: Letting go, new perspectives, sacrifice.
- **Meaning**: The Hanged Man can mean you need a pause to see things differently. It might suggest you surrender to the process and wait for clarity.
- **Advice**: Accept that sometimes you cannot rush ahead. Pause, reflect, and allow a new viewpoint to emerge.

4.15 Death (13)

- **Imagery**: A skeleton in armor, often riding a horse. There may be people or symbols of endings around it.
- **Theme**: Transformation, endings leading to beginnings.
- **Meaning**: Death is rarely about literal death. Instead, it is about transitioning from one phase to another. It can feel unsettling, but it often brings new growth.
- **Advice**: Let go of what no longer serves you. Embrace necessary changes so you can move forward.

4.16 Temperance (14)

- **Imagery**: An angel pouring liquid from one cup to another, usually standing with one foot on land and one foot in water.
- **Theme**: Balance, moderation, harmony.
- **Meaning**: Temperance suggests blending different factors to create something new and balanced. It can point to patience, cooperation, and finding the middle path.
- **Advice**: Avoid extremes. Take a measured approach and try to find peace between opposing elements in your life.

4.17 The Devil (15)

- **Imagery**: A horned figure with two people chained below him, sometimes resembling The Lovers card but in a darker setting.

- **Theme**: Temptation, materialism, feeling trapped.
- **Meaning**: The Devil can indicate you are stuck in negative patterns or giving in to harmful desires. It might show fear, addiction, or too much focus on material things.
- **Advice**: Recognize that you have the power to break free. The chains in this card are often loose, symbolizing that the "prisoner" can escape if they choose.

4.18 The Tower (16)

- **Imagery**: A tall tower struck by lightning, with people falling from it.
- **Theme**: Sudden change, upheaval, revelation.
- **Meaning**: The Tower can be shocking. It represents structures (physical or mental) that collapse to make way for truth. While this is a tough card, it can lead to a more honest path.
- **Advice**: Accept that some disruptions are necessary. After the shake-up, you can rebuild on stronger foundations.

4.19 The Star (17)

- **Imagery**: A woman pouring water on land and into a pond, often under a starry sky.
- **Theme**: Hope, inspiration, healing.
- **Meaning**: The Star is a welcome sign of calm after a storm. It encourages faith in the future and reminds you that guidance is available.
- **Advice**: Stay positive. Use this time to heal and wish upon your own guiding star. Trust in your direction.

4.20 The Moon (18)

- **Imagery**: A moon in the sky, often with a dog and a wolf howling, plus a path leading into the distance.
- **Theme**: Intuition, uncertainty, illusions.
- **Meaning**: The Moon can mean that things are not what they seem. There may be confusion or hidden truths. It also ties to dreams and the subconscious.
- **Advice**: Pay attention to your instincts. If the path seems unclear, take small steps and trust your inner compass.

4.21 The Sun (19)

- **Imagery**: A bright sun shining over a child or children, sometimes with sunflowers in the background.
- **Theme**: Joy, clarity, success.
- **Meaning**: The Sun is about positivity, confidence, and warmth. It often appears as a sign of good news or personal growth.
- **Advice**: Embrace happiness and let your true self shine. Share your joy with the world.

4.22 Judgment (20)

- **Imagery**: An angel blowing a trumpet while people rise from coffins.
- **Theme**: Rebirth, reflection, accountability.

- **Meaning**: Judgment can symbolize a call to awaken. It points to a time of self-evaluation, where you face your past actions and decide how to move forward.
- **Advice**: Be honest about what you have done or where you stand. Let go of guilt or old burdens and prepare for a new phase.

4.23 The World (21)

- **Imagery**: A figure (sometimes dancing or enclosed in a wreath), with symbols of the four evangelists (lion, bull, eagle, man) in the corners.
- **Theme**: Completion, success, unity.
- **Meaning**: The World shows that you have come full circle. A task or journey is complete, and you are ready to move on to the next level.
- **Advice**: Celebrate your accomplishments. Recognize that with endings come fresh starts.

4.24 Using the Major Arcana in Readings

When Major Arcana cards appear in a reading, they demand attention. A single Major Arcana card can influence the tone of the entire spread. For instance, if you draw **The Tower** next to Minor Arcana cards, it might suggest some kind of sudden shift in your daily life. If you draw **The Sun** with Minor Arcana cards, it can shine positivity on the rest of the reading.

Many readers see the Major Arcana as signifying spiritual or life-changing themes. You might ask yourself how that card's concept is relevant right now. Are you at a point of transformation (Death), healing (The Star), or reflection (Judgment)? Each card can act like a teacher, offering insights into your current life stage.

4.25 Reversed Major Arcana Cards

If you read with reversed cards, a Major Arcana reversal can modify the card's energy:

- It could mean you are resisting the lesson of that card. For example, reversed **The Fool** might suggest you are too scared to start something new.
- It could mean you need to look inward more. A reversed **The Hermit** might indicate you are avoiding alone time.
- It could mean the energy is present but not fully realized. A reversed **The Star** could imply hope is there, but you are not seeing it clearly yet.

Again, using reversed cards is an option, not a rule. Some readers simply interpret each card in both its positive and challenging lights, whether it is upright or reversed.

4.26 Tips for Learning the Major Arcana

1. **Start by Memorizing Names and Numbers**: Knowing the order (0 to 21) and the titles helps you see the flow of "The Fool's Journey."
2. **Notice the Common Stories**: Many decks show repeated themes like the sun, animals, or pillars. These help you remember the essence of each card.
3. **Write Down Keywords**: For each card, jot down a few keywords or short phrases. For Death, you might write "transformation" or "letting go."

4. **Look for Personal Connections**: Ask yourself if a particular card reminds you of a personal event or feeling. That memory can anchor the card's meaning in your mind.
5. **Practice Daily or Weekly**: Shuffle the Major Arcana and draw one card to focus on. Over time, you will build a bond with each card.

4.27 The Fool's Journey in Brief

Some teachers like to explain the Major Arcana as a story, where The Fool (0) is the main character:

- **Steps 1–7** (Magician to Chariot) can represent learning tools and building confidence in the external world.
- **Steps 8–14** (Strength to Temperance) can represent inner growth, facing fears, and balancing your energies.
- **Steps 15–21** (Devil to The World) can represent bigger tests, breakthroughs, and spiritual completion.

This narrative approach helps many students recall the flow from innocence to wisdom. It shows that each card is part of a journey, and life itself is a cycle of constant growth.

4.28 When a Reading Has Many Major Arcana Cards

If you do a spread (such as a Celtic Cross or a simpler three-card draw) and see multiple Major Arcana cards, it is a signal that something important is happening. It might mean:

- A major life transition (e.g., changing careers, moving homes, entering a new phase of life).

- A need to pay attention to big patterns or lessons, like learning to be more patient or trusting your intuition.
- A call to reflect on your personal values or spiritual direction.

Though it can feel intense, it also means you have a chance to learn significant lessons that can shape your future in a good way.

4.29 Balancing Major and Minor Insights

While the Major Arcana offers big themes, do not forget that day-to-day life matters too. The Minor Arcana shows how those themes play out in everyday steps. For example, if The Lovers (6) appears in a reading about relationships, look to the Minor Arcana cards to see what specific actions or attitudes might be relevant.

Perhaps you also see the **Two of Cups** (partnership) or the **Ten of Swords** (painful endings). These minor cards add depth to the bigger message of The Lovers. By blending both, you get a clearer picture of the advice the Tarot is giving.

Chapter 5: The Minor Arcana Cards

5.1 What Are the Minor Arcana?

The Minor Arcana make up the majority of a Tarot deck. There are **56 cards** in the Minor Arcana, divided into four suits. Each suit has **14 cards**: the **Ace** through the **10**, plus four **Court Cards** (Page, Knight, Queen, King). In this chapter, we will focus on the numbered cards—the Aces through the 10s. These cards often relate to our everyday experiences, challenges, and joys.

You can think of the Minor Arcana as the "daily stories" in life. If the Major Arcana covers major life themes and lessons, these 40 numbered cards (10 in each suit) show how those big themes might appear in smaller or more practical ways. For example, if the Major Arcana talk about transformation (like the Death card) or hope (like the Star), the Minor Arcana show how we might deal with those energies in our jobs, relationships, or personal projects.

Each suit focuses on a different area of life, such as emotions (Cups), work and money (Pentacles), thoughts and challenges (Swords), and creativity or passion (Wands). Learning the numbered cards gives you a clear map of how situations develop over time, from the fresh start of the Ace to the final stage of the 10.

5.2 Ace Through 10: A General Pattern

Before we look at each suit, let us talk about the general pattern from Ace through 10. While each suit has its unique meanings, the numbers themselves often carry a broad theme.

1. **Ace**: A beginning, spark, or fresh opportunity in that suit's area.
2. **Two**: A balance, partnership, or decision.
3. **Three**: Growth, expansion, or the first results of a plan.
4. **Four**: Stability or taking a pause to rest.
5. **Five**: A challenge, conflict, or disruption.
6. **Six**: Improvement, harmony, or rebalancing after difficulty.
7. **Seven**: Assessment, reevaluation, or deeper insight.
8. **Eight**: Action, movement, or progress.
9. **Nine**: Near completion, a peak moment.
10. **Ten**: Final outcome, completion, or full expression.

Keep this pattern in mind. Even though each card has its own unique flavor, you will notice these basic number meanings appear again and again.

5.3 Suit of Cups: Ace to 10

The **Cups** suit is linked to **Water**, symbolizing emotions, love, intuition, and relationships. When you see Cup cards, think about how you feel, how you connect with others, and how your heart is guiding you.

5.3.1 Ace of Cups

- **Meaning**: A fresh start in emotional matters. This could be new love, new friendship, or a wave of creative inspiration that touches your heart.
- **Advice**: Embrace openness and let your feelings flow. You might sense a positive emotional shift or a chance to deepen a bond.

5.3.2 Two of Cups

- **Meaning**: Often called the card of partnership or romance. It shows a meaningful connection between two people.
- **Advice**: Celebrate unity, whether it is a new friendship or a deeper commitment in love. Communicate openly to strengthen the bond.

5.3.3 Three of Cups

- **Meaning**: Joyful gatherings, celebrations, and friendship. Sometimes shows people raising cups in a toast.
- **Advice**: Take time to appreciate good times with loved ones. If you have been working hard, this card suggests sharing your happiness with friends.

5.3.4 Four of Cups

- **Meaning**: Feeling bored, unfulfilled, or stuck in a rut emotionally. The person on the card might not notice a new opportunity.
- **Advice**: Check if you are ignoring a gift or chance for happiness. Open your eyes to fresh possibilities you might be overlooking.

5.3.5 Five of Cups

- **Meaning**: Loss, sadness, or regret. Usually shows a figure focusing on spilled cups but missing the cups still standing.
- **Advice**: Acknowledge your sorrow, but remember there is still hope. Lift your head and see the support or opportunities that remain.

5.3.6 Six of Cups

- **Meaning**: Nostalgia, revisiting the past, childhood memories. May show two children sharing cups filled with flowers.
- **Advice**: Reflect on happy memories or reconnect with old friends. Just be mindful not to get stuck in the past; use those memories to bring warmth into the present.

5.3.7 Seven of Cups

- **Meaning**: Daydreaming, having many choices, or illusions. Sometimes too many options can cause confusion.
- **Advice**: Clarify what you really want. If you are lost in fantasies, take a step back and pick a realistic path forward.

5.3.8 Eight of Cups

- **Meaning**: Leaving something behind, searching for deeper meaning. Shows a figure walking away from stacked cups.
- **Advice**: If a situation no longer fulfills you, it might be time to move on. Courage is required to leave what is familiar for the unknown.

5.3.9 Nine of Cups

- **Meaning**: Often called the "wish card." Suggests contentment, emotional satisfaction, or personal fulfillment.

- **Advice**: Enjoy the good feelings. Be grateful for what you have. Celebrate your achievements, but avoid becoming complacent.

5.3.10 Ten of Cups

- **Meaning**: Emotional completion, family harmony, or deep happiness. May show a family under a rainbow of cups.
- **Advice**: Appreciate your supportive relationships. If you are seeking emotional well-being, this card can confirm that joy is possible.

5.4 Suit of Pentacles: Ace to 10

The **Pentacles** suit (sometimes called Coins) is linked to **Earth**, symbolizing money, work, health, and material stability. When you see Pentacle cards, think about practical matters, finances, and how you handle resources in your life.

5.4.1 Ace of Pentacles

- **Meaning**: A new financial opportunity, job offer, or chance for physical well-being. Can also indicate planting a seed for future success.
- **Advice**: Take advantage of this fresh start. Whether it is a new project or investment, nurture it carefully for long-term growth.

5.4.2 Two of Pentacles

- **Meaning**: Juggling finances, responsibilities, or tasks. Balancing multiple aspects of life.

- **Advice**: Stay flexible and adaptable. Prioritize what needs attention first. With good time management, you can handle everything on your plate.

5.4.3 Three of Pentacles

- **Meaning**: Teamwork, collaboration, or skill development. Often shows people working together on a building project.
- **Advice**: Do not be afraid to ask for help or share ideas. Together, you can achieve more than you would alone.

5.4.4 Four of Pentacles

- **Meaning**: Holding on tightly to resources or security. Can show a person gripping coins in fear of losing them.
- **Advice**: Saving money and being practical is good, but do not let fear of loss prevent you from sharing or enjoying life.

5.4.5 Five of Pentacles

- **Meaning**: Hardship, financial loss, or feeling left out in the cold. Often shows two figures walking in the snow outside a church.
- **Advice**: If you are struggling, remember that help may be available. Seek assistance and do not let pride isolate you.

5.4.6 Six of Pentacles

- **Meaning**: Generosity, charity, or balanced giving and receiving. A figure might be handing out coins to those in need.
- **Advice**: If you have the means, share with others. If you need help, do not be afraid to accept kindness. Balance is key.

5.4.7 Seven of Pentacles

- **Meaning**: Patience, waiting for a harvest, evaluating progress. Usually shows someone leaning on a tool, looking at growing pentacles.
- **Advice**: Keep nurturing your projects. Success often takes time. Assess what is working and adjust your plans if needed.

5.4.8 Eight of Pentacles

- **Meaning**: Hard work, honing a craft, or mastering a skill. A figure is often shown carefully crafting pentacles.
- **Advice**: Focus on improving your abilities. Dedication and practice lead to worthwhile results. Keep your eyes on the task.

5.4.9 Nine of Pentacles

- **Meaning**: Independence, self-reliance, and enjoying the fruits of your labor. Often shows a figure in a lush garden.
- **Advice**: Take pride in what you have earned. Reflect on your achievements. Treat yourself to a moment of pleasure or peace.

5.4.10 Ten of Pentacles

- **Meaning**: Long-term stability, family wealth, or a secure foundation for future generations.
- **Advice**: Value traditions and think about legacy. Plan for the long run to ensure ongoing stability and comfort for you and loved ones.

5.5 Suit of Swords: Ace to 10

The **Swords** suit is linked to **Air**, symbolizing thoughts, ideas, conflicts, and communication. When you see Sword cards, think about mental clarity, possible struggles, and the power of words or logic.

5.5.1 Ace of Swords

- **Meaning**: A new idea, sudden clarity, or mental breakthrough. The sword often pierces a crown, signifying victory in thought.
- **Advice**: Use this spark of insight to solve problems. If you need to speak up, do so clearly and honestly.

5.5.2 Two of Swords

- **Meaning**: Indecision, stalemate, or blocked emotions. Shows a figure blindfolded, holding two crossed swords.
- **Advice**: You might be avoiding a choice. Look at the facts and listen to your feelings. Removing the blindfold is the first step.

5.5.3 Three of Swords

- **Meaning**: Heartache, betrayal, or sorrow. Often shows a heart pierced by three swords.
- **Advice**: This card can be painful, but it also encourages you to face the hurt and begin healing. Do not bottle up sadness.

5.5.4 Four of Swords

- **Meaning**: Rest, recovery, or taking time out to reflect. May show a figure lying down with swords on the wall.

- **Advice**: If life has been intense, pause and recharge. Quiet your mind so you can return stronger.

5.5.5 Five of Swords

- **Meaning**: Conflict, unfair victory, or tension. Often depicts a person holding swords while others walk away.
- **Advice**: Winning at all costs could lead to regrets. Consider how your actions affect others. Maybe it is best to seek compromise.

5.5.6 Six of Swords

- **Meaning**: Transition, moving away from difficulty, sometimes traveling. A boat carries people across calmer waters.
- **Advice**: Moving on from a rough situation is key here. Healing takes time, but heading toward a safer place is the right choice.

5.5.7 Seven of Swords

- **Meaning**: Deception, trickery, or taking a cunning approach. Shows a figure sneaking away with swords.
- **Advice**: If you are tempted by shortcuts or dishonesty, think twice. Also, be cautious of others who might not be telling the full truth.

5.5.8 Eight of Swords

- **Meaning**: Feeling trapped, limited, or stuck in negative thinking. A figure is often blindfolded and surrounded by swords.
- **Advice**: You have more power than you think. The "cage" of swords might be partly self-imposed. Seek new perspectives to free yourself.

5.5.9 Nine of Swords

- **Meaning**: Anxiety, worry, or sleepless nights. Shows someone sitting up in bed, haunted by thoughts.
- **Advice**: Acknowledge your fears and find ways to cope. Talking to someone or seeking help can ease the burden.

5.5.10 Ten of Swords

- **Meaning**: Painful ending or betrayal. Often depicts a figure lying on the ground with swords in their back.
- **Advice**: As difficult as this seems, the worst is over. From this ending, you can rise again. Release old hurts and begin anew.

5.6 Suit of Wands: Ace to 10

The **Wands** suit (sometimes called Staffs or Rods) is linked to **Fire**, symbolizing creativity, ambition, passion, and personal power. When you see Wand cards, think of energy, drive, and what ignites your spirit.

5.6.1 Ace of Wands

- **Meaning**: A burst of inspiration, a new idea or project, creative energy.
- **Advice**: Seize this spark and let it guide you forward. If you have been waiting for motivation, here it is. Take the first step.

5.6.2 Two of Wands

- **Meaning**: Planning, making decisions about future actions. Sometimes shows a person holding the world in their hands.

- **Advice**: Look at the bigger picture. You have options—choose the path that aligns with your goals. Be bold.

5.6.3 Three of Wands

- **Meaning**: Expansion, waiting for rewards after taking initial steps. May show a figure watching ships on the horizon.
- **Advice**: You have started something promising. Keep an eye out for the next stage of growth. Trust that your efforts will pay off.

5.6.4 Four of Wands

- **Meaning**: Celebration, harmony at home, or reaching a milestone. Often depicts a festive scene with flowers.
- **Advice**: Enjoy the moment of success. Share your joy with others. This can also hint at gatherings or events that bring people closer.

5.6.5 Five of Wands

- **Meaning**: Competition, conflict, or a clash of wills. Often shows people with wands raised, seemingly battling or play-fighting.
- **Advice**: Conflict is not always bad. It can be a chance to learn or grow, but keep it respectful. Find ways to cooperate rather than fight.

5.6.6 Six of Wands

- **Meaning**: Victory, public recognition, or self-confidence. Shows a figure riding a horse in a parade.
- **Advice**: Celebrate your achievements. If you have succeeded, do not be shy about it. However, remain humble and grateful.

5.6.7 Seven of Wands

- **Meaning**: Standing your ground, defending your position. A figure stands on higher ground, fending off attackers.
- **Advice**: Protect what you have worked for. You may face challenges, but courage and persistence can help you overcome them.

5.6.8 Eight of Wands

- **Meaning**: Speed, action, quick communication. Often shows eight wands flying through the air.
- **Advice**: Events may start moving quickly. Stay alert and respond to opportunities that come your way. Do not delay.

5.6.9 Nine of Wands

- **Meaning**: Resilience, perseverance, and cautious hope. A figure stands wounded but determined.
- **Advice**: You are close to the finish line. Even if you are tired or skeptical, do not give up now. Trust your strength.

5.6.10 Ten of Wands

- **Meaning**: Burden, responsibility, feeling overloaded. A person struggles to carry a bundle of wands.
- **Advice**: Delegate or let go of extra weight if possible. You are almost there, but do not be afraid to ask for help.

5.7 How the Numbered Cards Work Together

When you look at the Minor Arcana numerically within each suit, you see a story:

- The **Ace** is the spark.
- The **Two** tries to balance or make a choice.
- The **Three** expands, while the **Four** rests or stabilizes.
- The **Five** is a test, the **Six** brings relief.
- The **Seven** contemplates deeper strategy, the **Eight** acts on it.
- The **Nine** is the height of the journey, and the **Ten** resolves that story, often preparing for the next cycle.

Each suit's storyline plays out differently due to the nature of Water (Cups), Earth (Pentacles), Air (Swords), or Fire (Wands). But the pattern of numbers is often consistent, helping you memorize or intuitively grasp what is going on.

5.8 Minor Arcana in Readings

When Minor Arcana cards appear in a spread, they often point to day-to-day matters. A person who draws many **Cups** might be dealing with emotional or relationship issues. Many **Pentacles** could mean work or money is on their mind. Many **Swords** might suggest mental stress or problem-solving. Many **Wands** could indicate a time of ambition and creative drive.

It is also helpful to notice repeated numbers. For example, if you see multiple "Fives," you might be facing conflicts or changes in different areas of life. If you see multiple "Tens," you might be completing several life chapters at once. Patterns like these can give you extra clues about the overall message.

5.9 Practical Exercise: Three-Card Draw With Minor Arcana

Here is a simple way to practice reading the numbered Minor Arcana:

1. **Shuffle** your deck thoroughly.
2. **Draw three cards** (focus on just the Minor Arcana for this exercise).
3. **Lay them out** in a row.
4. **Interpret** each card using its basic meaning, then see how they relate to each other.
   - For example: Suppose you draw the **Two of Pentacles**, the **Seven of Cups**, and the **Nine of Wands**.
   - **Two of Pentacles** might suggest juggling tasks or finances.
   - **Seven of Cups** might mean too many options or daydreaming.
   - **Nine of Wands** might mean you are tired but determined.
   - Putting them together, you could interpret that you feel overwhelmed by choices (Seven of Cups) and you are trying to manage them all (Two of Pentacles), which can be draining (Nine of Wands). The reading might advise you to narrow down your options, plan carefully, and stay strong until you reach your goal.

Chapter 6: Exploring the Four Suits

6.1 Why Focus on the Suits?

In Chapter 5, you learned the basics of the Minor Arcana numbered cards. Now, we are going to look more deeply at the **four suits** themselves—**Cups**, **Pentacles**, **Swords**, and **Wands**. Understanding each suit is crucial because it helps you see the "big picture" behind each card.

Each suit corresponds to a different **element** (Water, Earth, Air, Fire) and a different **area of life**. Recognizing these connections makes it easier to interpret the cards when they appear in a reading. For instance, if you see lots of Cup cards, you know emotions or relationships are front and center. If you see lots of Pentacles, practical matters like money or health likely need attention.

6.2 Suit of Cups (Element: Water)

6.2.1 Emotional Realm

Cups deal with **feelings**, **love**, **compassion**, and **intuition**. Water is fluid, always moving and changing, just like our emotions. In many decks, Cup cards have images of water—rivers, lakes, or flowing cups—to show the changing nature of our inner lives.

When you see Cup cards:

- You might be asked to reflect on your emotional well-being.

- Relationships (romantic, friendships, family) might be highlighted.
- There could be a call for empathy or creative expression.

6.2.2 Typical Strengths of Cups

- **Empathy**: Ability to understand others' feelings.
- **Creativity**: Artistic or imaginative thinking.
- **Compassion**: Kindness and a desire to help or heal.

6.2.3 Possible Weaknesses

- **Over-sensitivity**: Getting hurt easily or taking things personally.
- **Escapism**: Hiding in daydreams or fantasies instead of handling problems.
- **Moodiness**: Letting emotions rule decisions.

6.2.4 How to Spot a "Cup Situation"

If a reading is mostly Cups, you might be dealing with a love matter, an emotional choice, or a creative project. Perhaps you need to show more kindness or communicate your feelings clearly. Or maybe you are healing from an emotional wound and need time to nurture yourself.

6.3 Suit of Pentacles (Element: Earth)

6.3.1 Material Realm

Pentacles focus on the **physical world**: money, home, work, and health. Earth is solid and stable, associated with patience and long-term growth. In many decks, Pentacles appear as coins or discs, reminding us of life's material side.

When you see Pentacle cards:

- Your finances, job security, or health might be in the spotlight.
- You may need to pay attention to resources—like how you earn, spend, or invest.
- It could be time for practical planning and grounded decisions.

6.3.2 Typical Strengths of Pentacles

- **Practicality**: Good at dealing with real-world tasks and details.
- **Patience**: Willing to work steadily toward a goal.
- **Reliability**: Sticking to commitments and building a strong foundation.

6.3.3 Possible Weaknesses

- **Stubbornness**: Resistance to change or new ideas.
- **Materialism**: Focusing too much on money or possessions.
- **Laziness**: If Earth energy is blocked, it can lead to inactivity or lack of motivation.

6.3.4 How to Spot a "Pentacle Situation"

A reading with many Pentacles can hint at job changes, property matters, or the need for budgeting. You might also see it as a sign to focus on practical tasks—like updating your resume, planning a savings strategy, or working on your physical health.

6.4 Suit of Swords (Element: Air)

6.4.1 Mental Realm

Swords are about **thoughts**, **logic**, **communication**, and sometimes **conflict**. Air is invisible yet powerful, representing ideas, truths, and the power of the mind. Many Sword cards show tension, as the mind can be a place of stress or clarity.

When you see Sword cards:

- You may be asked to think logically or solve problems through strategy.
- There might be conflicts, debates, or important decisions that require clear thinking.
- Communication issues—such as an argument or misunderstanding—could need resolution.

6.4.2 Typical Strengths of Swords

- **Clarity**: Seeing truth and cutting through confusion.
- **Reason**: Using logic to make fair decisions.
- **Assertiveness**: Speaking up for your beliefs or defending your ideas.

6.4.3 Possible Weaknesses

- **Overthinking**: Worrying excessively or getting stuck in "analysis paralysis."
- **Harshness**: Words can hurt, so Sword energy can be cutting or blunt.
- **Conflict**: Instead of cooperation, a strong Swords presence might indicate fighting or rivalry.

6.4.4 How to Spot a "Sword Situation"

Lots of Swords in a spread could mean you are in a tense situation requiring sharp judgment. It might also mean it is time to speak your truth, or that you are dealing with mental stress. Learning to communicate openly can help ease potential conflicts.

6.5 Suit of Wands (Element: Fire)

6.5.1 Creative Realm

Wands represent **inspiration**, **ambition**, **passion**, and **personal drive**. Fire is warm, energetic, and sometimes unpredictable, much like the spark of creativity or motivation. Wand cards often show growth, excitement, or even drama.

When you see Wand cards:

- You might be urged to pursue your passion or follow a new idea.
- It could be a time of high energy, requiring you to stay focused so you do not burn out.
- You might need to show courage or take a bold step in a project.

6.5.2 Typical Strengths of Wands

- **Enthusiasm**: Infectious energy that can inspire others.
- **Confidence**: Belief in yourself and willingness to take risks.
- **Leadership**: Ability to spark action or lead a team toward a vision.

6.5.3 Possible Weaknesses

- **Impulsiveness**: Acting before thinking can cause chaos.
- **Burnout**: Going full speed all the time can drain energy.
- **Self-Centeredness**: Focusing only on personal glory without regard for others.

6.5.4 How to Spot a "Wand Situation"

If you see many Wands, you are probably in a busy or exciting phase. You might be launching a new venture, feeling creative sparks, or challenging yourself with ambitious goals. Just be sure to manage your energy well.

6.6 How the Suits Interact

One of the exciting parts of reading Tarot is noticing how the suits interact in a spread. For example:

- **Cups + Pentacles**: Emotional fulfillment combined with practical security. Maybe you find a job that aligns with your heart or you gain a new friendship at work.
- **Swords + Wands**: High mental activity plus a burst of creative energy. This can be great for problem-solving but can also be tense if arguments flare.
- **Cups + Swords**: Emotions meet logic. You may need to find the balance between what your heart feels and what your mind knows.
- **Pentacles + Wands**: Using your energy and passion to build something real and lasting. Think of an entrepreneur who has both ambition (Wands) and a solid business plan (Pentacles).

When you see a mix of suits, look at which suits appear most. That can tell you which areas of life are currently the most active, and which might be playing a supporting role.

6.7 Elemental Dignities (Optional)

Some Tarot readers use **elemental dignities** to see how cards might support or weaken each other:

- **Compatible Elements**: Water (Cups) and Earth (Pentacles) often work smoothly together, as do Fire (Wands) and Air (Swords).
- **Incompatible Elements**: Water (Cups) and Fire (Wands) can clash, as can Earth (Pentacles) and Air (Swords).
- **Neutral Elements**: Some suits neither help nor hinder each other significantly.

This is an extra layer of interpretation. If you want to keep it simple, you can ignore elemental dignities. If you love detail, they can add another dimension to your readings.

6.8 Recognizing Suit Patterns in a Reading

Sometimes, you will see a reading where almost every card comes from the same suit. For example, if you pull five cards and four of them are Wands, it could mean you are in an extremely energetic, creative time. However, it might also suggest you are ignoring your emotions (Cups), your finances (Pentacles), or your mental clarity (Swords).

In a balanced reading, you might see a mix of suits, indicating you are handling various parts of life. A reading with no Cups at all, for instance, might warn you to check if you are emotionally distant. A reading with no Pentacles might mean you are ignoring practical details. These suit "gaps" can be just as telling as the suit that shows up the most.

6.9 Examples of Suit-Focused Questions

When you shuffle the Tarot deck, you can ask specific questions related to a suit:

1. **Cups**: "How can I improve my relationship with a friend?" or "What emotional blockages do I need to clear?"
2. **Pentacles**: "Which steps can I take to improve my finances?" or "How can I find more stability in my career?"
3. **Swords**: "What truth am I avoiding?" or "How can I solve this conflict at work?"
4. **Wands**: "How can I reignite my passion for my hobby?" or "Which creative project should I focus on right now?"

You do not have to remove the other suits from the deck, but focusing on a suit's theme when you ask a question can help you see your concerns more clearly.

6.10 Suit Case Studies

Let us look at a few mini case studies where the suits provide insight.

6.10.1 A Job Dilemma (Pentacles + Swords)

Imagine you are unhappy at work. You draw three cards:

- **Eight of Pentacles** (hard work, skill development)
- **Five of Swords** (conflict, tension)
- **Two of Pentacles** (juggling, decisions)

Interpretation: You might be putting in a lot of effort (Eight of Pentacles), but conflicts with coworkers or a tense environment (Five of Swords) is weighing on you. The Two of Pentacles suggests you are struggling to balance tasks or perhaps deciding if you should stay or look for a new job. Notice all these cards point to practical or mental stress—Pentacles for daily labor and Swords for conflict. The reading encourages you to weigh your options carefully and consider if further skill-building or a job switch is best.

6.10.2 A Creativity Block (Wands + Cups)

Let us say you feel stuck writing a short story. You draw three cards:

- **Seven of Wands** (defensiveness, standing your ground)
- **Ace of Cups** (emotional new beginning)
- **Nine of Wands** (perseverance, near the finish line)

Interpretation: The Wands here show you are battling creative blocks (Seven of Wands, Nine of Wands) but still have the drive to continue. The Ace of Cups suggests tapping into fresh emotional inspiration—perhaps writing about a personal experience or something that moves your heart. Even though you feel tired (Nine of Wands), your new wave of feeling (Ace of Cups) can push you through.

6.10.3 A Love Question (Cups + Major Arcana)

Although we are focusing on suits, you might see a Major Arcana card in the mix. Suppose you ask about your love life and draw:

- **Two of Cups** (partnership, romance)
- **The Lovers** (major life choice in love)
- **Ten of Cups** (emotional fulfillment, family)

Interpretation: The heavy presence of Cups plus **The Lovers** (Major Arcana) suggests a significant romantic moment. Maybe you are deciding to take a relationship to the next level. The Ten of Cups points to a happy outcome if you choose wisely. Notice that the suits can work seamlessly with the Major Arcana to give a full picture.

6.11 Balancing the Suits Within Yourself

Each of us has a personal "suit" we relate to most. Some people are very emotional (Cups), others are super practical (Pentacles), while some are strong communicators (Swords) or natural leaders (Wands). Overemphasizing one suit can throw us off balance. For instance, focusing only on career success (Pentacles) might leave you neglecting your relationships (Cups) or your spiritual side.

A valuable Tarot lesson is that we need all four elements to thrive:

- Water for emotional well-being
- Earth for stability and security
- Air for clear thinking
- Fire for passion and drive

If you notice one suit is consistently missing from your readings, it might be time to pay attention to that area of life.

6.12 Simple Spread: Four-Suit Check-In

Here is a spread you can try to assess your balance across the four suits:

1. **Shuffle** your entire deck well.
2. **Draw four cards**, one for each suit. Place them in four positions, labeled Cups, Pentacles, Swords, and Wands.
3. **Interpret** each card in the context of that suit's energy:
    - **Cups Position**: What is the state of my emotions or relationships?
    - **Pentacles Position**: What is the state of my work, finances, or health?
    - **Swords Position**: What is the state of my thoughts, communication, or conflicts?
    - **Wands Position**: What is the state of my drive, ambition, or creativity?

This spread can give a quick snapshot of where you stand in each elemental area. If any card suggests trouble or concern, you know which part of your life needs extra care.

6.13 Suit Colors and Symbols

Different decks use color schemes to highlight each suit:

- **Cups**: Often associated with blues or greens (water colors).
- **Pentacles**: Commonly shown with browns or earthy tones.
- **Swords**: Typically silver, gray, or sometimes stormy colors.
- **Wands**: Often red, orange, or golden to reflect fiery energy.

Symbols within each suit might include:

- **Cups**: Water, fish, waves, or moon imagery.
- **Pentacles**: Gardens, coins, fields, or material objects like houses.
- **Swords**: Birds (for Air), clouds, or storms.
- **Wands**: Flames, branches, leaves, or desert scenes.

Pay attention to these details; they help reinforce the elemental feeling of the suit, making your readings more immersive and intuitive.

6.14 Avoiding Suit Stereotypes

While suits do have core energies, remember that people are complex. Not every Cup card means someone is "always weepy," and not every Sword card means a harsh conflict. Tarot is about nuance. A person can be strong in Swords (very intellectual) but still have a loving heart. A reading might reveal the sides of a person or situation that are most relevant at that moment, rather than describing their entire personality forever.

6.15 Reversed Suit Cards

If you read reversed cards (when a card appears upside-down), you can interpret the suit's energy as blocked, delayed, or misapplied. For instance:

- A reversed **Cup** card might hint at repressed emotions or emotional overwhelm.

- A reversed **Pentacle** card could indicate financial struggles or laziness.
- A reversed **Sword** card might show confusion or a sharp tongue causing harm.
- A reversed **Wand** card could mean burnout or misplaced aggression.

Some readers prefer to keep all cards upright and consider both positive and negative possibilities. Whether you use reversals is up to you, but if you do, it can add extra detail to your readings.

6.16 Using the Suits in Real-Life Scenarios

Here are some everyday examples of how paying attention to suits can guide you:

1. **Preparing for a Test (Swords)**: If you draw many Swords, you might need more study, clarity, and focus on communication.
2. **Starting a Fitness Routine (Pentacles + Wands)**: Earth (Pentacles) for practical routine, Fire (Wands) for the motivation to keep going.
3. **Improving Family Bonds (Cups)**: Water (Cups) is crucial for nurturing love, empathy, and understanding.
4. **Launching a Business (Wands + Pentacles)**: You want ambition (Wands) plus solid planning (Pentacles). If Swords appear, it might advise careful contracts or clear communication.
5. **Resolving a Friendship Dispute (Cups + Swords)**: Emotions (Cups) are involved, but open dialogue (Swords) is needed.

Thinking in terms of suits can simplify your reading process. You can see right away which "element" is most active and respond accordingly.

6.17 Suit Meditations

Some Tarot readers like to do meditations focusing on one suit. For example, you might:

1. Take all the **Cups** cards out of the deck.
2. Spread them in front of you.
3. Gently gaze at each card, noticing how water themes appear.
4. Reflect on your emotions and how they shift each day.

You can do this with Pentacles, Swords, or Wands as well. It is a good way to absorb the unique energy of each suit and see patterns in the artwork or symbolism.

6.18 Suit Journaling

Another fun exercise is to keep a "suit journal." Each week, focus on one suit:

- **Week 1 (Cups)**: Track your emotions. Notice times when you felt compassion or needed emotional support.
- **Week 2 (Pentacles)**: Look at your spending habits, diet, or daily routines. Did you stay grounded?
- **Week 3 (Swords)**: Observe your thoughts and communications. Did you speak your mind? Did you handle conflicts well?
- **Week 4 (Wands)**: Check your energy levels, motivation, and creative ideas. How did you act on them?

By doing this, you train yourself to recognize these four energies in your everyday life, making it easier to interpret them when you see them in the cards.

6.19 Common Suit Misunderstandings

1. **Wands = Only Creativity?**: While Wands do represent creativity, they also represent general energy and ambition. It is not limited to artistic pursuits. It can be any passion or goal.
2. **Cups = Only Romance?**: Cups are about all emotions, not just love. They can point to friendships, family feelings, or even your relationship with yourself.
3. **Pentacles = Just Money?**: Pentacles include health, home life, and even personal values—anything in the physical or material realm.
4. **Swords = Always Bad?**: Swords can be tough, but they also bring truth, wisdom, and clarity. They help cut away confusion.

Chapter 7: Working with Court Cards

7.1 Who Are the Court Cards?

So far, we have looked at the Major Arcana (which deal with big life themes) and the numbered cards in the Minor Arcana (Ace through 10 in each suit). Now, it is time to discuss the **Court Cards**, which are sometimes called the "face cards" of the Tarot. There are **four Court Cards** in each suit:

1. **Page** (sometimes called Princess)
2. **Knight** (sometimes called Prince)
3. **Queen**
4. **King**

Since there are four suits (Cups, Pentacles, Swords, Wands) and each suit has four Court Cards, that gives us **16 Court Cards** in total. These cards often stand for **people** (including you), or for **personality traits** or **energies**. That makes them a bit different from the numbered cards, which usually refer to situations, events, or feelings.

Reading Court Cards can be tricky. Sometimes you might look at a card like the **Queen of Swords** and wonder if it is telling you about a woman you know, or if it is pointing to your own mental clarity. Or, you might see the **Knight of Wands** and think, "Is this card talking about a friend who loves to travel, or is it suggesting I need to be more adventurous?" One key to handling these questions is to stay open to multiple interpretations. Over time, you will get a sense of when the Court Card points to a real person and when it symbolizes a certain approach, attitude, or behavior.

7.2 Court Card Ranks: Page, Knight, Queen, King

Even though the names sometimes vary from deck to deck (for example, "Princess" instead of "Page"), the **four ranks** generally keep the same idea:

7.2.1 Pages

- **Basic Meaning**: Youth, learning, curiosity, fresh starts in the realm of that suit.
- **Personality Traits**: Pages are like beginners or students. They can be eager, excited, or naive. They often show a spark of interest in a new subject or skill.
- **Questions to Ask**: Does this card suggest you (or someone else) should be open to learning? Is there a young person in your life who fits this description?

7.2.2 Knights

- **Basic Meaning**: Action, movement, the drive to pursue goals. Each Knight moves differently based on the suit's element.
- **Personality Traits**: Knights tend to be adventurous, active, and sometimes impulsive. They can represent strong energy, a sense of questing, or chasing something.
- **Questions to Ask**: Is this card urging you to take action? Does it point to a person who is bold and ready for challenges?

7.2.3 Queens

- **Basic Meaning**: Mastery of the suit's inner qualities, nurturing, wisdom, or maturity in that area.
- **Personality Traits**: Queens are often seen as caretakers and leaders, but in a more internal or nurturing way than Kings. They shape and guide the suit's energy.

- **Questions to Ask**: Are you being called to care for something or someone? Is there an influential person in your life who embodies these traits?

7.2.4 Kings

- **Basic Meaning**: Full authority, leadership, or control over the suit's domain. Kings channel the suit's energy outward with confidence.
- **Personality Traits**: Kings often appear as decision-makers, protectors, or directors. They can be strong, but they must be careful not to become overbearing.
- **Questions to Ask**: Where in your life are you (or someone else) stepping into a leadership role? How can you manage that power wisely?

7.3 Court Cards in Each Suit

Now, we will look at how each rank (Page, Knight, Queen, King) behaves in the context of its **suit** (Cups, Pentacles, Swords, Wands). Remember, each suit has an element and a domain of life:

- **Cups = Water (emotions, relationships)**
- **Pentacles = Earth (money, work, practical matters)**
- **Swords = Air (thoughts, communication, conflict)**
- **Wands = Fire (creativity, ambition, passion)**

7.3.1 Court of Cups

1. **Page of Cups**:
    - **Meaning**: Youthful emotions, new emotional or creative ideas, a message of love or friendship.
    - **Traits**: Imaginative, sensitive, possibly shy or dreamy.

- **Scenario**: Could be a young person discovering their artistic talents or someone who needs to express feelings more openly.

2. **Knight of Cups**:
   - **Meaning**: Action guided by emotions, romantic gestures, or following one's heart.
   - **Traits**: Charming, idealistic, sometimes wearing "rose-colored glasses."
   - **Scenario**: Might represent a person who follows their passion or someone who brings a proposal or invitation.

3. **Queen of Cups**:
   - **Meaning**: Deep emotional understanding, compassion, healing.
   - **Traits**: Empathetic, supportive, intuitive, protective in a gentle way.
   - **Scenario**: Could be someone who listens well, offers comfort, or teaches others to trust their hearts.

4. **King of Cups**:
   - **Meaning**: Emotional maturity, calm leadership through empathy, balancing feelings with logic.
   - **Traits**: Wise, compassionate, stable under emotional pressure.
   - **Scenario**: Might point to a mentor who gives caring advice or someone who leads with kindness in a challenging situation.

7.3.2 Court of Pentacles

1. **Page of Pentacles**:
   - **Meaning**: A new start in work, health, or practical matters. Curiosity about money or a new trade.
   - **Traits**: Eager to learn skills, detail-oriented, grounded.

- Scenario: Could be an intern or student who is serious about developing a craft.
2. **Knight of Pentacles**:
    - **Meaning**: Steady progress, reliability, dedicated effort.
    - **Traits**: Hardworking, cautious, sometimes slow to act but consistent.
    - **Scenario**: May symbolize someone who works methodically to reach goals, or a situation that moves slowly but surely.
3. **Queen of Pentacles**:
    - **Meaning**: Nurturing prosperity, providing comfort, focusing on physical well-being of oneself and loved ones.
    - **Traits**: Generous, practical, good at managing resources.
    - **Scenario**: Might describe someone who runs a household efficiently or gives excellent financial or health advice.
4. **King of Pentacles**:
    - **Meaning**: Mastery over the material realm—wealth, security, business success.
    - **Traits**: Stable, protective, enjoys the good life, may be stubborn.
    - **Scenario**: Could point to a boss who offers financial wisdom or a family member who ensures everyone is taken care of materially.

7.3.3 Court of Swords

1. **Page of Swords**:
    - **Meaning**: A curious mind, new ideas, a message of truth, or the start of a mental challenge.
    - **Traits**: Quick-witted, talkative, sometimes a bit blunt or nosy.

- **Scenario**: Could be a student, a gossip, or someone who is learning to communicate more clearly.
2. **Knight of Swords**:
    - **Meaning**: Swift action, charging ahead with logic, possibly conflict or cutting words.
    - **Traits**: Brave, outspoken, impulsive in speech or thought.
    - **Scenario**: Might symbolize a person who rushes into debates or challenges, or an event that requires fast thinking.
3. **Queen of Swords**:
    - **Meaning**: Sharp intellect, honesty, independence, setting clear boundaries.
    - **Traits**: Witty, fair-minded, can appear cold but values truth greatly.
    - **Scenario**: Could be someone who gives tough love or advice, or a call to be more direct and logical in a tough situation.
4. **King of Swords**:
    - **Meaning**: Authority in intellectual matters, strong leadership, rational decision-making.
    - **Traits**: Analytical, firm but just, may lack tolerance for emotional drama.
    - **Scenario**: Might point to a judge, a lawyer, or a manager who leads through logic and strategy.

7.3.4 Court of Wands

1. **Page of Wands**:
    - **Meaning**: New spark of creativity, eagerness to explore, message about an exciting opportunity.
    - **Traits**: Enthusiastic, curious, might be restless or easily bored.

- **Scenario**: Could be a childlike energy discovering a new passion or someone about to start a creative journey.
2. **Knight of Wands**:
    - **Meaning**: Bold action, adventure, possibly impulsiveness.
    - **Traits**: Confident, energetic, loves challenges, may be hot-tempered or impatient.
    - **Scenario**: Might symbolize a person who loves to travel, an athlete, or a risk-taker who jumps at chances.
3. **Queen of Wands**:
    - **Meaning**: Warm leadership, charisma, the ability to inspire others.
    - **Traits**: Independent, passionate, friendly, good at networking.
    - **Scenario**: Could be someone who lights up a room and encourages everyone to do their best, or a moment where you need to show your boldness.
4. **King of Wands**:
    - **Meaning**: Visionary leadership, drive, grand ambitions.
    - **Traits**: Inspiring, confident, sometimes a bit dominating.
    - **Scenario**: May point to an entrepreneur, a community leader, or any person who rallies others to accomplish a big dream.

7.4 How to Know If a Court Card Represents a Person or an Energy

A common question is, "Does this Court Card represent me, someone else, or a general energy?" Here are some tips:

1. **Context of the Reading**: If your question is about how to handle a project at work, and you draw a **King of Pentacles**, it might suggest adopting a mindset of practicality and careful planning. If your question is "Who can I ask for help?" and you draw the **King of Pentacles**, it might indicate a financially stable or business-savvy person in your life.
2. **Age and Personality**: Sometimes, the card's rank gives you a clue about the person's maturity. A **Page** might suggest someone younger or someone new to the topic. A **King** might suggest a mature figure with experience. This is not always about literal age—someone can be "young at heart."
3. **Suit Energy**: Look at the suit's domain. If you are reading about emotional conflicts in your family, a **Queen of Cups** could be your supportive mother, or it could mean you need to offer compassionate leadership.
4. **Intuition**: Trust your gut. If you see the **Knight of Wands** and instantly think of your adventurous best friend, that might be correct. Tarot reading often involves quick intuitive hits.

7.5 Court Cards in Spreads

7.5.1 A Three-Card Example

Let us say you do a three-card reading asking, "How can I move forward in my creative hobby?" and you draw:

1. **Page of Wands** (Past)
2. **Knight of Pentacles** (Present)
3. **Queen of Cups** (Future)
- **Page of Wands (Past)**: You started your hobby with excitement and childlike curiosity.

- **Knight of Pentacles (Present)**: Now it is time to be consistent and hardworking, focusing on building real skills day by day.
- **Queen of Cups (Future)**: If you do so, you will find deeper emotional fulfillment. You may become a caring mentor to others who share your creative interest.

7.5.2 Multiple Court Cards in a Reading

When many Court Cards appear, it can suggest that many people are involved in your situation. For instance, if you are asking about a family conflict, you might see the **Queen of Swords**, the **Knight of Wands**, and the **King of Cups**, indicating different personalities in the household. Another approach is that these different Court Cards represent aspects of yourself—perhaps you need the logical mind of the Queen of Swords, the drive of the Knight of Wands, and the compassion of the King of Cups to find a solution.

7.5.3 Reversed Court Cards (Optional)

If you use reversed cards (where the card appears upside down), a reversed Court Card might point to the negative or blocked side of that personality:

- A reversed **Queen of Cups** could be overly emotional or manipulative.
- A reversed **Knight of Swords** could rush in without thinking, causing chaos.
- A reversed **King of Wands** might be domineering or inflexible.

If you do not use reversals, you can still consider both positive and challenging aspects of each Court Card. They are not always perfect—each rank in each suit can have its flaws.

7.6 Recognizing Court Cards in Real Life

Think of people you know. Can you spot a **Knight of Pentacles** type—a friend who is always methodical, saving money, planning carefully? Do you know a **Queen of Wands** type—someone who dazzles at parties and leads with creative passion? When you see these traits in real life, it helps you read the cards better.

Here is a short exercise:

1. Write down the names of four people in your life.
2. Try matching each one to a Court Card. Think about whether they fit the Cups, Pentacles, Swords, or Wands energy, and whether they feel more like a Page, Knight, Queen, or King.
3. Note why you chose that card for them. This practice can help you remember the cards more naturally.

7.7 Court Cards as Personal Archetypes

Some people view the Court Cards as **archetypes**—universal patterns of behavior or personality. For instance:

- The **Page of Swords** is the curious student, always asking questions.
- The **Knight of Cups** is the romantic hero who follows his heart.
- The **Queen of Pentacles** is the nurturing homemaker or the wise caretaker of resources.
- The **King of Wands** is the visionary leader who inspires others.

In your own life, you might be a "Page of Cups" when you start learning to paint, or a "Queen of Swords" when you lead a team meeting and need to be direct. Recognizing these archetypes can help you see yourself and others more clearly.

7.8 Practical Tips for Reading Court Cards

1. **Look at Surrounding Cards**: A Court Card next to, say, the **Three of Swords** might suggest heartbreak. Is the Court Card showing how to cope with it or the person causing it?
2. **Consider the Question**: If your question is "Which part of myself do I need to develop?" then a Court Card is more likely to represent an aspect of you than someone else.
3. **Age and Gender**: Traditional Tarot art often shows male Kings and female Queens. However, the energy can be present in any gender or age. A "King of Cups" type could be a 20-year-old woman if she acts with mature emotional leadership. Tarot is flexible.
4. **Multiple Meanings**: A single Court Card might represent a person, an energy, a message, or a future role you must step into. Keep an open mind.

7.9 Court Cards as Messengers

Because Pages are often shown carrying letters or messages in some decks, some readers see them as **messengers**. For example:

- **Page of Cups**: An emotional or creative message ("I love you," "I have a new art idea").
- **Page of Pentacles**: A practical message about money, school, or health.
- **Page of Swords**: An intellectual message, a new idea, or even gossip.

- **Page of Wands**: An exciting proposal or adventurous opportunity.

Knights can also bring messages, but they are more about taking action. For instance, the **Knight of Wands** might suggest a sudden trip or bold move.

7.10 Court Card Exercises

7.10.1 Single Card Reflection

Pick a Court Card randomly. Spend 10 minutes journaling about it:

- What do you see in the picture?
- What is the suit's element telling you?
- How might you describe this card as a person?
- What might you learn from that person?

7.10.2 Roleplaying

Imagine you are the card. If you draw the **Queen of Cups**, pretend you are that nurturing, empathetic figure. How would you handle a problem with your neighbor? How would you talk to a sad friend? This can help you understand the card's energy on a personal level.

7.10.3 Court Card Scavenger Hunt

During your day, look for people or situations that match each Court Card. If your coworker is being direct and logical in a meeting, you might think, "That is a Queen of Swords moment." Or if you see a student excitedly starting a new project, that is a "Page of Wands" scene.

Chapter 8: Choosing the Right Tarot Deck

8.1 Why Does the Deck Matter?

Tarot decks come in many styles, themes, and sizes. You might have seen decks with classic medieval-like images, or ones with bright modern art, or even decks that feature animals or mythical creatures. While they all share the same **78-card structure** (22 Major Arcana, 56 Minor Arcana), the *look* and *feel* of each deck can vary a lot.

Choosing the right deck is important because the artwork and symbolism can deeply influence how you connect with the cards. If you are drawn to gentle, pastel colors and simple images, you might not feel comfortable reading a deck with very dark or gothic art. Likewise, if you love bold, dramatic designs, you might find simpler decks boring.

Some readers own **multiple decks** for different moods, readings, or clients. Others pick one deck and stick to it for years. Either way is fine. The key is to find at least one deck that resonates with you, because when you enjoy the images, you are more likely to read the cards with confidence and clarity.

8.2 Traditional vs. Modern Decks

8.2.1 Rider-Waite-Smith (RWS)

One of the most popular Tarot decks in the world is the **Rider-Waite-Smith (RWS) Deck**, first published in 1909. Created by **A. E. Waite** and illustrated by **Pamela Colman Smith**, it has classic, bright images. Many beginners start with this deck because most Tarot books and resources reference its artwork. The Minor Arcana cards show people and scenes (not just suit symbols), making it easier to memorize meanings through visual storytelling.

8.2.2 Thoth Deck

Another well-known deck is the **Thoth Tarot**, created by **Aleister Crowley** and painted by **Lady Frieda Harris**. It has a different style, with detailed, sometimes abstract images and more esoteric symbols. Some card names differ from the RWS tradition (for example, "Justice" might be "Adjustment"). This deck can be powerful but might feel more complex for absolute beginners.

8.2.3 Marseille Deck

The **Tarot de Marseille** is one of the oldest styles, originating in Europe centuries ago. Many Marseille decks have simpler, more traditional woodcut-style artwork. The Minor Arcana typically feature repetitive suit symbols (like pips in playing cards) rather than full scenes. Some readers enjoy the historical charm, while others find it less intuitive because there are fewer pictures to interpret in the Minors.

8.2.4 Modern Themed Decks

Today, there is a huge variety of **themed decks**:

- Animal-themed (e.g., cats, ravens, wolves)
- Fantasy-themed (e.g., dragons, fairies)
- Cultural-themed (e.g., focusing on a specific mythology or region)
- Art-style decks (e.g., watercolor, minimalist, steampunk)
- Pop-culture decks (e.g., TV show or movie inspirations)

If you love cats, a Cat Tarot deck might be perfect. If you adore Japanese artwork, there are decks inspired by manga or ukiyo-e prints. The advantage of these modern decks is that they can spark excitement and help you stay engaged.

8.3 Factors to Consider When Choosing a Deck

8.3.1 Artwork and Style

Look at sample images from the deck, especially the Major Arcana and a few Minor Arcana cards. Ask yourself:

- Do I like the colors and the way people or symbols are drawn?
- Can I imagine using these pictures to tell a story or get insights?

8.3.2 Size and Card Stock

Tarot decks come in various sizes, from large "oracle-sized" cards to smaller, more standard sizes. If you have small hands, a huge deck might be hard to shuffle. Also, pay attention to the card stock's thickness and finish. Some decks have glossy coatings, others have a matte finish. Think about whether you want cards that slide easily or ones with more grip.

8.3.3 Guidebook or Little White Book

Most decks come with a **Little White Book (LWB)** or a detailed guidebook. These explain the artist's view on each card's meaning. Some guidebooks are very short, just a few words per card. Others offer long descriptions, stories, or even journaling prompts. If you want more guidance, look for a deck with a more substantial book.

8.3.4 Cultural or Symbolic Alignment

Some decks lean heavily on certain spiritual traditions or mythologies. Make sure you feel comfortable with that. If a deck uses Egyptian symbols but you have no interest in Egyptian mythology, you might find it less intuitive. If you love Celtic lore, a Celtic-themed deck might bring the cards alive for you.

8.3.5 Budget

Deck prices vary. Simple decks with a small booklet can be cheaper, while special edition decks with fancy boxes and thick guidebooks cost more. You do not have to break the bank to find a good starter deck. Many well-made decks are quite affordable.

8.4 Where to Buy Tarot Decks

1. **Local Bookstores or Metaphysical Shops**: You can often see decks in person before buying. This helps you feel the card size and see the artwork up close.

2. **Online Retailers**: Websites provide sample images. You might find reviews from other buyers.
3. **Direct From Creators**: Some artists publish their decks independently. Buying directly can support the creator and sometimes include special extras like signed cards.
4. **Used Decks**: Some people enjoy secondhand decks for their unique history. Others prefer brand-new decks so they can form their own bond.

8.5 Myths About Deck Ownership

8.5.1 "You Must Be Gifted a Deck"

A common myth says you should never buy your own deck—someone else must give it to you. While that is a fun tradition, there is no rule that says you cannot buy your own. Many readers select and purchase their decks happily. It is important to choose a deck that speaks to your heart.

8.5.2 "You Can Only Have One Deck at a Time"

Some people do just fine with a single deck. Others collect dozens. There is no rule limiting how many decks you can own. It is about what feels comfortable and practical for you.

8.5.3 "One Deck Is Always the Best"

No single deck is the "best" for everyone. Each person has different tastes. Some love the classic RWS images, others prefer modern styles. The best deck is the one that *you* feel drawn to and can read confidently.

8.6 Building a Personal Connection With Your Deck

Once you choose a deck, you might want to form a bond with it. Here are some ideas:

1. **Look Through Every Card**: Take time to flip through the deck slowly. Notice your first impressions.
2. **Journal**: Write down any thoughts, feelings, or questions about each card.
3. **Daily Draw**: Pull one card each day. Reflect on how it might apply to your life. This helps you learn and connect.
4. **Meditate**: Some people like to meditate with a specific card, imagining themselves in the scene.
5. **Storage and Care**: Keep your deck in a pouch, box, or cloth that you like. This shows respect and helps maintain its condition.

Remember that these steps are optional. There is no mandatory ritual. Just do what makes you feel comfortable and linked to your deck.

8.7 Switching Decks or Working With Multiple Decks

Over time, you may feel called to try another deck. Perhaps you found something new that you love, or maybe you want a deck with different artwork for different types of questions. Many readers rotate between decks. For example:

- **Deck A** for relationship or emotional readings (maybe a soft, dreamy style).
- **Deck B** for career or financial questions (maybe a deck with practical, earthy art).
- **Deck C** for creative brainstorming (maybe a deck with bold, funky designs).

Working with multiple decks can keep things fresh. It also broadens your symbolic vocabulary because each deck has its own artistic interpretation.

8.8 Signs You Have Found "Your" Deck

Sometimes, people talk about finding a deck that feels like a perfect match—like meeting a new friend who shares your interests. You might notice:

- **Immediate Attraction**: The images grab your attention and excite you.
- **Ease of Reading**: Even without reading a guide, you sense what each card means.
- **Emotional Response**: Some cards give you goosebumps or make you smile.
- **Synchronicities**: Strange coincidences happen, like pulling the same card that matches your daily experiences.

If you feel a strong connection, that deck might be your "go-to" or primary reading deck. But do not worry if you do not feel that spark right away—sometimes the bond grows as you practice.

8.9 Overcoming Deck Discomfort

What if you buy a deck and realize you do not like the images? Or you feel uneasy about certain symbols? Here are some solutions:

1. **Give It Time**: Some decks grow on you after repeated use. Try daily draws for a week or two.
2. **Modify the Deck**: Some readers trim the borders or rewrite card names if the original style bothers them.
3. **Trade or Gift**: If you truly dislike the deck, you can trade with another Tarot enthusiast or gift it to a friend who might love it.
4. **Use It for Art or Study**: You can keep the deck as part of your collection for reference or study. There is no rule that says you must read with every deck you own.

8.10 Deck Interviews and Spreads

Some Tarot readers like to do a special "deck interview spread" when they first get a new deck. This is a fun way to learn about the deck's personality. A simple version might include three cards:

1. **What will you teach me?**
2. **How should I work with you?**
3. **What is our shared strength?**

It sounds playful, but it can spark insights and help you bond with your new deck.

8.11 Taking Care of Your Deck

Once you have your chosen deck(s), consider how you will care for them:

- **Keep Them Clean**: Wash your hands before handling the cards if they are easily smudged.
- **Protect Them from Damage**: Store in a safe place, away from moisture or sunlight that could fade the images.
- **Respectful Handling**: Shuffle gently if you do not want bent corners. If you like riffle shuffling (like playing cards), that is fine, but be aware it can cause wear over time.

Some people perform rituals like passing the cards through incense smoke or letting them sit under moonlight to "clear old energy." These are personal choices. The main goal is to keep your deck physically safe and in a condition that feels good to you.

8.12 Digital or App-Based Decks

With modern technology, there are many Tarot apps that allow you to do readings on your phone or tablet. These apps can be convenient, especially when you are on the go. They often include guidebooks, card-of-the-day features, and even journaling options.

However, some people feel that physical cards have a special energy. If you love the tactile experience of shuffling and flipping cards, you might prefer physical decks. It is okay to use both! Apps can be a good supplement or a handy way to practice.

8.13 Deck Collecting

Be warned: Tarot deck collecting can become a hobby in itself! There are so many beautiful decks that it is easy to want them all. Before you know it, you might have a shelf full of Tarot boxes. If that makes you happy and you can afford it, there is nothing wrong with collecting. Just make sure you do not feel guilty if you do not use each deck all the time.

8.14 Matching Decks to Questions or Clients

If you read for others, you might choose different decks depending on the person or the topic:

- A gentle, uplifting deck for someone who is nervous or dealing with emotional stress.
- A bold, edgy deck for someone who loves drama and strong visuals.
- A minimalistic deck if you want to focus purely on the symbolism without lots of extra details.

Even if you only read for yourself, you can experiment by using a certain deck for career questions and a different deck for spiritual growth.

8.15 Crafting Your Own Deck

Some dedicated Tarot enthusiasts eventually design their own decks. You do not need to be a professional artist—some people do it purely for personal use, cutting out images they like or drawing stick figures that represent the card meanings. Creating your own deck can be a powerful way to understand the Tarot deeply. Each card becomes a personal project of symbols and color choices.

If you ever feel called to do this, do not worry about perfection. It is your own personal expression. You can also keep a digital scrapbook of images that represent each card before you print or draw them.

8.16 Overcoming New Deck Anxiety

It is normal to feel overwhelmed when you get a new deck. You might worry you will not understand the images or that it is too different from what you are used to. Here are some calming thoughts:

- **Remember the Core Structure**: Even if the art is unusual, the deck still has 22 Major Arcana and 56 Minor Arcana. The suits are still Cups, Pentacles, Swords, and Wands (or their equivalents).
- **Use What You Know**: The basic meanings of The Fool, The Magician, and so on will likely still apply, even if the picture is different. Look for the key symbols.
- **Learn the Creator's Perspective**: Skim the guidebook to see how the deck's creator interprets each card. You might discover new layers of meaning you enjoy.

8.17 Sample Deck Exploration

To see how you might explore a new deck, imagine you bought a nature-themed Tarot. You open it and see that each suit is linked to a season:

- **Cups** = Spring (water, rain, flowers)
- **Pentacles** = Autumn (earth, harvest)
- **Swords** = Winter (cold air, snow)
- **Wands** = Summer (fire, heat, sunshine)

You flip through the cards:

- The **Fool** might show a young traveler on a fresh green path.
- The **Wheel of Fortune** might show a cycle of the four seasons.
- The **Page of Cups** could be a springtime scene with new blossoms.
- The **King of Wands** might be in the middle of a blazing summer sun.

Seeing these images, you realize the deck's theme is about growth, cycles, and environmental harmony. You then ask yourself: "Do I connect with the seasons? Does this imagery bring me clarity?"

8.18 Deck Dedication

Some Tarot readers do a "dedication" ritual when they get a new deck. This could be as simple as lighting a candle and saying, "I welcome this deck into my practice. May our work together bring insight and compassion." It is not required, but can be a nice way to mark the beginning of your journey with the deck.

Chapter 9: Caring for Your Tarot Deck

9.1 Why Care for Your Tarot Deck?

In earlier chapters, we looked at choosing the right Tarot deck and working with its images. Now, let us explore how to **care for your Tarot deck**. Why does care matter? For many readers, a Tarot deck is more than just pieces of printed cardboard—it is a companion on a personal or spiritual journey. Keeping your deck in good shape helps it last longer. It can also make your readings feel more special and focused.

You might wonder if caring for a deck means you need to follow strict rules. There are no hard-and-fast rules that everyone must follow. However, there are some helpful guidelines you can use. Think of it like caring for a favorite book or a treasured stuffed animal: you do not want it to get dirty or torn, and you might keep it in a place of honor so you can find it easily. In this chapter, we will look at different ways people protect and store their decks, keep them clean, and show respect to them.

9.2 Physical Care: Keeping Your Deck Safe

9.2.1 Clean Hands and Clean Surfaces

One of the simplest things you can do is make sure your hands are clean before touching your cards. If your hands are oily, sticky, or dusty, that residue might transfer to the cards. Over time, this can make them look worn out or cause discoloration. Also, try to shuffle on a clean surface—like a table or cloth—so you do not scrape dirt or crumbs into the edges.

9.2.2 Storing Your Deck

Once you are done reading, you want to store your deck somewhere it will be protected from direct sunlight, moisture, or extreme heat. Some readers like to:

- **Keep it in the original box**: This is often sturdy and was made to fit the deck exactly.
- **Use a cloth bag or pouch**: Many Tarot shops sell special pouches for cards. Some are plain; others have artistic designs.
- **Wrap it in a scarf**: A simple piece of cloth can protect the cards from dust and from shuffling around too much in a drawer.
- **Use a wooden box**: If you like a solid container, you can find small wooden boxes or decorative tins that fit a Tarot deck well.

Pick a method that feels right to you and matches your style. The main goal is to avoid letting the deck get bent or scratched. If you travel with your deck, you might want something sturdy to prevent damage in your bag.

9.2.3 Avoiding Direct Sunlight

Long exposure to sunlight can fade the colors on your cards, especially if the deck has bright or delicate artwork. Keep your cards away from windows where intense sun might shine for hours. Some people do like to place cards briefly in the sun for special reasons (like a short "cleansing" ritual), but be mindful of how strong the sun is and how long you leave them there.

9.2.4 Keeping Your Deck Dry

Moisture is another enemy of paper. If your house is very humid, consider storing your deck with a small packet of silica gel (often found in shoe boxes or other packaging) to reduce moisture. Do not place your deck near sinks, bathtubs, or anywhere spills are common. If you accidentally spill water (or any liquid) on your deck, blot it gently with a towel and let the cards air dry. Do not try to speed things up with a hairdryer, because the heat could warp them.

9.3 Handling the Cards Gently

9.3.1 Shuffling Styles

We discussed shuffling techniques briefly before, but it is good to revisit how to handle your deck gently. Some people do **riffle shuffling** (like how casino dealers shuffle playing cards), bending the deck in half. This can cause wear along the edges or create creases if you are not careful. If you like the riffle shuffle, do it softly, without forcing the deck too much.

Another method is the **overhand shuffle**, where you hold the deck in one hand and use the other hand to pull small groups of cards to the front. This is gentler. Some readers also do a **"spread and mix"** shuffle: they spread the cards in a big circle on the table and swirl them around. This method keeps the cards mostly flat and reduces bending.

9.3.2 Letting Others Touch Your Cards

A common question is whether to allow someone else to handle your deck. Some readers feel that letting others touch their cards can transfer unwanted energy. Others do not mind at all, because they see the deck as a tool that can adapt easily. This is a personal choice.

- **If you prefer to keep your deck personal**: You might shuffle and draw the cards yourself, and not hand them to the other person.
- **If you do not mind**: You could let someone else shuffle or cut the cards if it helps them feel connected to the reading.

If you ever feel your deck's "energy" is off after someone else handles it, you can do a simple cleanse (see the next section on energetic care).

9.3.3 Dealing With Wear and Tear

No matter how careful you are, your deck might show signs of use over time—slightly frayed edges, a tiny crease, or some faded spots. This does not mean your deck is ruined. Some readers love the look of a well-worn deck, saying it carries memories of past readings. If a card becomes too damaged to use, you might look into replacing the entire deck or see if the publisher offers individual replacement cards (though that is rare). Alternatively, you could retire that deck as a sentimental keepsake and buy a fresh copy.

9.4 Energetic Care: Cleansing and Recharging

9.4.1 What Is "Energetic Care"?

Some people like to think of a Tarot deck as having an energy or vibe. While this is not a fact in the same sense as "do not let your cards get wet," it is a belief many find meaningful. They see the deck as a tool that absorbs or reflects the reader's feelings and the situations it is used for. If that resonates with you, then you might want to "cleanse" or "reset" your deck's energy from time to time.

9.4.2 Simple Ways to Cleanse

There are many ways to energetically clear your deck. None are mandatory, but here are some popular methods:

1. **Knocking or Tapping**: Hold the deck in one hand and gently knock on it with your other hand's knuckles. Imagine you are knocking out old energy.
2. **Breathing**: Shuffle or hold the cards, then blow gently over the top or edges of the deck. Visualize your breath clearing away lingering thoughts.
3. **Moonlight**: Some readers like to leave their deck by a window overnight during a full moon or new moon. They feel this refreshes the deck's energy.
4. **Sound**: Use a small bell, a tuning fork, or even a short piece of calming music. Place the deck near the sound and let the vibrations wash over it.
5. **Smoke or Incense**: Carefully pass the deck through the smoke of sage, palo santo, or incense. Be mindful of fire hazards and do this in a well-ventilated area.

Choose the method that feels right to you. If none of these appeal to you, it is perfectly fine to skip them. Tarot can work just fine without rituals.

9.4.3 When to Cleanse

You can cleanse your deck anytime you feel it might help. Some readers cleanse after a stressful reading, after someone else has used their deck, after a long period without using it, or whenever they sense the deck feels "heavy." Others stick to a schedule, like at the start of each month. Listen to your instincts.

9.5 Bonding With Your Deck

9.5.1 Spending Time Together

Bonding is not just about energetic cleansing; it is also about familiarizing yourself with every card. One way to bond is to go through each of the 78 cards, one by one, and note any immediate impressions. You can ask yourself:

- "How do I feel when I see this image?"
- "Is there a story unfolding in the picture?"
- "Are there symbols or colors that stand out?"

You might keep a journal for these observations. Over time, you build a personal relationship with each card, making your readings more intuitive.

9.5.2 Daily Card Draws

Another bonding exercise is pulling a single card every morning or night. Look at it, notice its details, and think about how it might relate to your day. This helps you see the cards in action. If the deck is brand-new, daily draws are a friendly way to get acquainted without overwhelming yourself.

9.5.3 Deck Interview Spread

We mentioned the idea of a "deck interview" in a previous chapter, but it is worth revisiting in the context of caring for your deck. An interview spread might have questions like:

1. "How can we work together best?"
2. "What strengths do you bring?"
3. "What challenges might arise as we learn?"
4. "How can I respect and care for you?"

By drawing one card for each question, you get a playful introduction to your deck's personality—if you enjoy that kind of imaginative approach.

9.6 Rituals and Respect

9.6.1 Personal Touches

Some readers create small rituals around their cards. For example:

- **Lighting a candle** before picking them up.
- **Saying a short phrase** or prayer, like "I seek guidance for my highest good."
- **Placing crystals** like clear quartz or amethyst on or near the deck.

These actions can set a calm mood and remind you that Tarot is a mindful practice. Do you need to do these things? No. If they feel comforting or meaningful, go for it. If not, keep it simple.

9.6.2 Reading Environment

How you treat your deck can also reflect in the environment you create for readings. A clear, uncluttered table can help you focus. If you are in a noisy place, you might want headphones with gentle music or simply wait until it is quieter. Showing respect to your deck often means giving it (and yourself) a pleasant space to work in. We will talk even more about setting up a reading space in the next chapter, but it is good to remember that the deck might read "more smoothly" for you when the environment is calm.

9.7 Keeping a Deck Log

9.7.1 Why Log Your Deck Usage?

Some Tarot readers keep a "deck log" or "deck journal," where they note each reading's date, time, question, and the cards that appeared. They may also write down impressions or outcomes that happened later. This log can help you see how often you use the deck, which cards show up frequently, and how your interpretations evolve.

9.7.2 Possible Log Sections

- **Readings and Questions**: List the question and the spread used.
- **Cards Pulled**: Write down each card that came up.
- **Interpretations**: Briefly note your initial thoughts.
- **Follow-Up**: A few days or weeks later, see if anything in your life lined up with your reading.
- **Deck Feelings**: Did the deck feel easy to read or did you feel a block?

Having a deck log can help you bond with your deck and also track how your readings progress over time. You might realize, for example, that you kept getting the **Knight of Wands** whenever you asked about your new hobby, showing that consistent energy in your life.

9.8 Rotation and "Deck Rest"

9.8.1 Taking Breaks

Sometimes, you might use a deck intensively for a while—maybe giving readings to friends every day. You might reach a point where you feel you want to give that deck a rest. Some people store the deck for a week or two to let it "recharge" or to avoid personal burnout. Then, when you bring it out again, it feels fresh.

9.8.2 Rotating Decks

If you own multiple Tarot decks, you can rotate between them. Perhaps you use Deck A for personal readings, Deck B for readings with friends, and Deck C for creative brainstorming. By switching up the deck, you also reduce wear and tear on any one deck. Each deck can have its own "personality," and you might discover that certain decks excel at certain types of questions.

9.9 Handling Travel and Public Readings

9.9.1 Traveling with Your Deck

If you like to keep your Tarot deck with you on trips, consider a durable box or a padded pouch. If the deck is going into luggage, protect it so it will not get crushed by heavy items. Some readers have a "travel deck"—maybe a smaller Tarot version that is easier to carry around. Always be aware of the place you are visiting: in some cultures or situations, Tarot might be misunderstood, so be mindful of local norms.

9.9.2 Public or Outdoor Readings

If you do readings in a park, at a café, or at a fair, watch out for wind, food spills, or rowdy crowds. A rubber-backed cloth can help keep the cards in place. You might also bring an extra cloth or bag to protect them if you need to leave the table. If someone is curious about your reading and wants to handle the cards, you decide if that is okay. The main thing is to keep your deck safe from accidental damage.

9.10 Myths About Deck Care

9.10.1 "You Must Wrap Your Deck in Silk"

You might hear that you **must** wrap your deck in black silk, keep it under your pillow, or never let it see daylight. Such advice can be interesting traditions, but they are not universal rules. If you like the idea of silk or any other cloth, that is perfectly fine. If you prefer a simple cardboard box, that is okay too. The deck will not be "angry" or refuse to work if you do not follow these customs.

9.10.2 "Never Let Anyone Else Shuffle Your Cards"

Another myth is that letting someone else shuffle or touch your cards will ruin them or bring bad luck. Some readers do prefer that nobody else touches their deck, but others happily let friends shuffle. It is a personal choice. If you are comfortable sharing, do so. If not, kindly explain that you prefer to handle the cards yourself.

9.10.3 "Decks Can Get Cursed if They Are Not Cleansed"

The idea of a deck being cursed is more of a superstition. Yes, a deck can feel "off" if you have had a negative experience, but that does not mean you are doomed. A short cleansing ritual or simply taking a break can refresh the energy. Tarot is ultimately a tool, and you have the power to shape your experience with it.

9.11 Troubleshooting Common Deck Issues

1. **Warped Cards**: If your deck bends slightly, you can gently bend them back or place them under a heavy book for a few days.

2. **Sticky Edges**: Sometimes new decks have stiff edges that stick. Gently separate each card and lightly shuffle. If you want, you can use a soft cloth to rub the edges.
3. **Reversed Cards Getting Mixed**: If you do not read reversals but find some cards turned upside down, go through the deck and correct them after each reading. Keep track as you shuffle.
4. **Missing Cards**: Occasionally, a card might slip under a couch or table. Do a count (78 total) after big readings or if you suspect one is gone. If truly lost, you might need a replacement deck.

9.12 Embracing Personal Preferences

By now, you can see there are many ways to care for a Tarot deck. Some readers do elaborate rituals, store their deck in fancy silk, and refuse to let anyone else even breathe on it. Others keep it casual, treat the deck just like a well-loved paperback book, and it works great for them. The important thing is to find an approach that suits your comfort level and helps you feel confident while reading. If you are gentle with your deck physically, it can last many years. If you also do energetic cleanses and bonding activities, you may find your readings feel more in tune.

Chapter 10: Setting Up Your Reading Space

10.1 Why the Reading Space Matters

Imagine trying to do detailed homework in a crowded, noisy room where people are shouting and a TV is blaring. It is hard to concentrate. In a similar way, **where** you do your Tarot readings can affect how clear your mind is. You do not need a huge fancy altar or a room filled with special decorations, but it helps to have a comfortable, uncluttered spot that allows you to focus on the cards.

A reading space can be as simple as your kitchen table, or as elaborate as a dedicated room with candles, music, and crystals. The key is to create an environment where you feel **relaxed**, **open-minded**, and **prepared** to interpret the messages the cards offer.

10.2 Choosing the Location

10.2.1 A Quiet Corner at Home

Many people read Tarot in their homes. You might pick a corner of your living room, bedroom, or study area where you can sit without too many distractions. If you share your home with family or roommates, let them know you need a little privacy. This does not have to be a strict rule, but letting them know helps them avoid interrupting you.

- **Table or Surface**: You need enough space to lay out the cards. A desk, table, or even the floor can work if it is clean and comfortable.

- **Chair or Cushion**: Ensure you can sit in a stable, relaxed posture. If you prefer sitting on the floor, use a cushion to avoid discomfort.

10.2.2 Outdoor Spaces

Some readers love the energy of nature. If you have a quiet backyard, a patio, or a nearby park that is not too crowded, you can do a reading outdoors. Listen to birds, feel the breeze, and let the fresh air inspire you. Just remember to watch out for wind that could blow your cards away, and keep an eye on any damp grass or surfaces.

10.2.3 Public Areas

You can also do Tarot readings in cafes or libraries, though it might be trickier to find privacy. Some people enjoy reading in a local coffee shop for the cozy atmosphere. Others set up at a festival or fair if they are reading for the public. In these cases:

- **Choose a quiet corner** if possible.
- **Keep your belongings secure**—especially your deck.
- **Be ready for curiosity**: People might come up and ask about the cards.

10.3 Ensuring Comfort

10.3.1 Temperature and Lighting

If your reading space is too hot, cold, or poorly lit, you might get distracted and rush your readings. Aim for:

- **Comfortable Temperature**: Use a fan if it is warm, or a blanket if it is chilly.

- **Proper Lighting**: Natural light is often ideal, but if it is nighttime, have a lamp that is bright enough to see details on the cards without straining your eyes.

10.3.2 Seating Support

If you plan to read for more than a few minutes, a supportive chair helps prevent back or neck strain. If you are on the floor, you can use a floor cushion or a small stool. Your posture can influence how long you can comfortably focus on the reading.

10.3.3 Minimal Distractions

Try to reduce things that might pull your attention away from the cards. This could be:

- **Turning off or silencing your phone** (unless you need it for a timer or notes).
- **Closing noisy windows** if traffic or construction sounds bother you.
- **Politely asking others** to give you some quiet time if they can.

10.4 Atmosphere and Ambiance

10.4.1 Lighting Options

Some Tarot readers love to create a special mood. If that interests you, consider:

- **Candles**: The soft flicker can be calming. Just make sure to practice fire safety, especially if you have curtains or papers around.

- **Fairy Lights**: Small LED lights can add a magical glow without the worry of an open flame.
- **Dim Lighting**: If you enjoy a more mysterious feel, dim the room a bit—but keep enough light to see the cards clearly.

10.4.2 Scents and Incense

Some people burn incense or use essential oil diffusers. Scents like lavender or sandalwood can promote relaxation. If you or anyone nearby is sensitive to smells, you might skip this step. You can also choose unscented candles. The idea is to pick a scent that makes you feel calm, not overwhelmed.

10.4.3 Background Music

Gentle music or nature sounds can help you relax. You could play soft instrumental tunes or ambient tracks. Avoid loud or distracting lyrics that might pull your attention away from the reading. If you prefer total silence, that is also fine. The aim is to create a supportive background that does not compete with your focus on the Tarot.

10.5 Using a Tarot Cloth or Mat

10.5.1 Why Use a Cloth?

A Tarot cloth is a piece of fabric (like a small tablecloth or scarf) that you lay out before placing your cards. Some people love using one because it:

- **Protects cards** from dirt or scratches.
- **Defines a clear reading area** and feels like a mini "sacred space."
- **Adds beauty** to the setup and can help keep you organized.

10.5.2 Choosing a Cloth

You can find Tarot-specific cloths in online shops or metaphysical stores, often with designs like moons, stars, or Celtic knots. But you do not need a special one. A simple piece of fabric you already have can work just as well, as long as it is clean and large enough to hold the layout you want. Some readers prefer darker cloths that make the cards pop; others like colorful or themed fabrics.

10.5.3 Folding and Storing

When finished, some people wrap their deck in the cloth. Others fold it neatly and keep it separately. If you do keep your deck wrapped in the cloth, it can protect the cards from dust, as we discussed in the previous chapter.

10.6 Setting Intentions

10.6.1 Clearing Your Mind

Before you start drawing cards, it can help to take a moment and clear your thoughts. You might:

- **Close your eyes** and take a few slow, deep breaths.
- **Visualize** yourself surrounded by a calm, positive light.
- **Repeat a phrase** like, "I am open to clear guidance," or "Let me see the truth in these cards."

This does not have to be long or fancy. Even 10 seconds of mindful breathing can help you shift your focus from daily tasks to the reading at hand.

10.6.2 Personal or Spiritual Practices

If you have a spiritual tradition, you can say a short prayer or call on a sense of higher guidance. If you are not spiritual, you could just center yourself mentally by thinking, "I am ready to explore these questions." The key is to be **present**. Setting an intention can turn an ordinary moment into a special ritual, making the reading feel more purposeful.

10.7 Organizing Your Tools

10.7.1 What Tools Might You Have?

Beyond the cards themselves, you might have:

- **Guidebook**: If you need to look up meanings or references.
- **Notebook or Journal**: To jot down your impressions or the card spread.
- **Pen or Pencil**: For quick notes.
- **Crystals, Stones, or Talismans**: If you like having them nearby for positive energy.
- **Timer or Clock**: Helpful if you do not want to lose track of time, especially if you are reading for someone else and want to keep the session focused.

10.7.2 Keeping Things Handy

Having these items within reach helps you avoid jumping up mid-reading to search for a pen or rummage for your guidebook. You can keep a small basket or tray near your reading space with everything ready. This way, once you begin the reading, you can stay in the flow without interruption.

10.8 Reading for Others in Your Space

10.8.1 Seating Arrangements

If someone visits you for a reading, think about how you will sit. Many readers like to sit across from the other person, with the table (and the Tarot layout) between them. This way, both can see the cards. Some prefer sitting side by side, especially if they want to share the same perspective of the card images.

10.8.2 Making Guests Comfortable

Offer your guest a comfortable chair. If they like a certain type of background music, you can accommodate that as long as it does not distract you. Ask if they want anything to drink (like water or tea). Being a welcoming host can help them relax, which often leads to a more open and helpful reading.

10.8.3 Privacy and Boundaries

If a reading might touch on personal or sensitive topics, ensure that other people in the home know not to interrupt. Close the door or choose a part of the house where others are less likely to pop in. This respects your guest's privacy. Also, if your reading space is in a public café, it might be harder to keep the conversation private, so you and your guest might speak softly or choose a corner table.

10.9 Traveling Reading Setup

10.9.1 Portable Items

If you give Tarot readings outside your home—for example, at a local fair or a friend's event—you can still create a cozy mini-space. Bring:

- A **foldable cloth or mat** to spread on any table.
- A **small sign** that says "Tarot Readings" if appropriate.
- Any items that help set the mood (like a single candle or crystal), as long as they are safe and allowed.

10.9.2 Dealing With Noise

At public events, you cannot always control the noise level or the music being played. Do your best. You might ask to be placed in a corner away from loudspeakers or the biggest crowd. Some readers learn to focus in all sorts of conditions. A quick mental check-in—breathing deeply—can help you stay calm even in a busy environment.

10.9.3 Handling Curious Onlookers

In a public setting, strangers may gather around to watch. If your guest wants a private reading, kindly ask onlookers to give you space. If your guest is okay with an audience, be mindful of what personal details you share. Some people do quick "showcase readings" for watchers, but keep deeper details private for individual sessions.

10.10 Your Personal Touches

10.10.1 Decorations and Themes

Over time, you might personalize your reading area to match your style. You could:

- Hang artwork on the wall that inspires you.
- Place a small statue or figurine that feels symbolic.
- Use table runners or pillows with designs you love.

This does not have to be expensive. Even a single flower in a small vase can make the space feel special. Let your creativity guide you.

10.10.2 Seasonal or Festive Ideas

Some readers change their reading space according to the season—putting up pastel colors in spring, golden tones in autumn, or fairy lights in winter. You might add seasonal decorations or scents (like cinnamon in the fall). This can keep the space fresh and keep you excited about your Tarot practice all year round.

10.11 Dealing With Distractions and Interruptions

10.11.1 Phone Calls and Messages

We live in a world full of technology. If your phone rings during a reading, decide how you want to handle it. Many readers silence their phones, but if you are expecting an important call, let your reading partner know in advance. You could say, "I am expecting a quick call, so I might need to pause for a moment." That way, they understand it is not a lack of respect.

10.11.2 Pets or Children

Pets might jump on the table or children might run around if you are reading at home. If possible, you can set up your space in a room with a closed door. Or, if having a pet around is actually soothing for you and does not disturb the reading, you can let them stay. Just be aware that not everyone is comfortable with animals sniffing or stepping on the cards.

10.11.3 Unexpected Visitors

Sometimes a neighbor might drop by or a family member might barge in. If you can, calmly let them know you are in the middle of a session and will catch up with them afterwards. You can put a small sign on the door—"In Session" or "Do Not Disturb"—if that helps.

10.12 Ending the Reading and Clearing the Space

10.12.1 Gathering the Cards

After the reading is done, take a moment to gather the cards carefully. If you have used multiple decks or oracle cards, put each deck back in its box or bag so you do not mix them up. Some readers like to give the deck a quick shuffle to "reset" it. If you had a big spread, you might also take a photo or write down which cards appeared so you can refer back to it later.

10.12.2 Tidying Up

Put away any items you used—guidebooks, notebooks, crystals, or incense holders. Blow out candles if they are still burning (safety first!). Fold your Tarot cloth, then store it and the deck in their usual spot. This small act of tidying can feel like you are closing the ritual. It also helps keep your reading space ready for next time.

10.12.3 Thanking the Space or Deck

Some readers like to say a quick thank-you, either silently or aloud: "Thank you for the guidance" or "I appreciate this space." It can be a small moment of gratitude that ends the reading on a positive note. If gratitude practices do not resonate with you, that is okay—do whatever feels right.

10.13 Troubleshooting Space Issues

1. **Limited Space**: If you live in a tiny apartment or share a room, a small fold-up table or even your bed can suffice. You can use a tray as a makeshift table.
2. **Noisy Environment**: Earplugs or noise-canceling headphones with soft music can help. Or wait for a quieter time, like early morning or late evening.
3. **No Table**: If you absolutely have no table, reading on the floor is fine—just use a cloth to protect the cards.
4. **Curious Housemates**: Explain gently that Tarot reading is important to you and you need some quiet time. Set boundaries.

10.14 Keeping Your Space Special

Having a consistent reading spot can strengthen your Tarot practice. Over time, your mind may associate that corner or table with the act of reading, making it easier to slip into the right mindset. You do not need to do anything fancy. Simply being consistent—using the same candle, cloth, or arrangement—can help trigger your focus. Think of it like a routine that tells your brain, "Now it is Tarot time."

Chapter 11: Shuffling and Handling Techniques

11.1 Why Shuffling Matters

When you read Tarot, you might be tempted to rush straight to pulling cards for your question. But there is an important step that helps you connect with the cards and clear your mind: **shuffling**. Shuffling is more than just randomizing your deck. It can be a moment of reflection or a small ritual that focuses your thoughts on the question or situation at hand.

Some people see shuffling as a "bridge" between your everyday life and the symbolic world of the Tarot. Others simply view it as a practical way to ensure the cards are not in a predictable order. Either way, it is worth spending some time learning different shuffling methods. You can choose the style that feels comfortable and respectful to your cards.

11.2 Basic Principles of Shuffling

11.2.1 Randomizing the Cards

The main purpose of shuffling is to make the final order of the cards unpredictable. If you have used the deck before, it might still be arranged in a pattern, or certain cards might be together. Shuffling breaks any arrangement so that each card has an equal chance of turning up. This allows the reading to feel fresh and not pre-determined by a previous layout.

11.2.2 Focusing on Your Question

Shuffling can also be a way to **focus your mind** on a specific question. You might think about your topic as you shuffle. For instance, if you are asking, "How can I resolve this conflict at work?" you can hold that thought gently in your mind, letting your hands move the cards while your mind zeroes in on the problem. This brief meditation can help you approach the reading with clarity.

11.2.3 Respect for the Cards

Some readers see Tarot cards as tools that deserve care. Shuffling gently is one way to show respect. If you aggressively bend or throw the cards around, you might damage them or treat them like cheap playing cards. Treating them kindly can help you feel more connected. Of course, it is also okay to do a brisk shuffle if that is what suits your personality—just be aware of physical wear and tear.

11.3 Common Shuffling Methods

11.3.1 Overhand Shuffle

The **overhand shuffle** is one of the simplest techniques. Here is how you do it:

1. **Hold the deck** in your dominant hand, supporting the bottom and one side with your fingers.
2. **Use your other hand** to lift a small group of cards from the top and let them drop back onto the deck.
3. **Repeat** this process, pulling off small or medium chunks of cards and letting them fall in front or behind the deck in your hand.

This shuffle looks like you are sliding cards off the top and letting them drop. It is gentle on the cards, and beginners often find it easy to control. You can do this several times, mixing up how many cards you pick up each time.

Pros:

- Easy to learn.
- Less risk of bending cards.
- Quiet and subtle.

Cons:

- May not feel random enough to some people, especially if you move very few cards each time.
- Can take longer to feel thoroughly mixed.

11.3.2 Riffle Shuffle

The **riffle shuffle** is what you often see in casinos with playing cards. You split the deck roughly in half, then bend each half so the corners interleave. Then you let the cards spring together, creating a distinctive "shuffle" sound. Here is how to do a gentle riffle:

1. **Divide the deck** into two roughly equal stacks.
2. **Hold each stack** with your thumbs along the inner edges and your fingers at the outer edges.
3. **Bend each half** slightly upward.
4. **Release the corners** slowly so they interlace.
5. **Push** or gently bridge the two halves together, letting the cards slide into a single stack.

Some Tarot readers worry about bending or damaging the cards, especially if the deck is large or thick. To avoid problems, use a light touch. Do not force a deep bend. Also, be mindful that many Tarot decks are bigger than standard playing cards, so it may be harder to do a riffle shuffle if you have small hands.

Pros:

- Thorough randomization in fewer shuffles.
- Satisfying sound and feel.

Cons:

- Possible bending or creasing of cards if done aggressively.
- Harder for beginners or those with small hands.

11.3.3 Pile or "Cowie" Shuffle

Another method is to **deal the cards into several piles** and then gather them back up in a different order. For example:

1. Decide on how many piles (say 4 or 5).
2. Deal the deck out one card at a time: first card goes to pile 1, second card goes to pile 2, etc., cycling through the piles.
3. Once you have dealt the entire deck, **pick up the piles** in a random order.

This method is slower, but it can break up patterns effectively. It is also a good choice if your hands get tired from overhand or riffle shuffles. You can combine it with other shuffling techniques to get an even more random order.

Pros:

- Very thorough in redistributing the cards.
- Gentle on the deck.
- Easy for people with small hands.

Cons:

- Takes more time.
- Might feel less fluid or graceful than other methods.

11.3.4 Wash or "Scramble" Shuffle

In this method, you "wash" or scramble the cards on a flat surface. You have likely seen children do this with playing cards. It is straightforward:

1. **Spread** the deck face-down on the table in a big circle or pile.
2. **Use your hands** to swirl the cards around in random directions.
3. **Gather** them back into a single stack.

This shuffle is especially good for beginners or for large groups of people who want to each get a hand in mixing. However, you need a clean, flat surface and enough space. Make sure you do not scratch or damage the card edges by pressing too hard or swirling over rough surfaces.

Pros:

- Simple, no special technique required.
- Can be fun in a group setting.
- Thorough mixing if done long enough.

Cons:

- Cards can get scuffed or bent if not careful.
- Requires a bigger surface area.

11.4 Shuffling Duration and Intuition

One question that comes up often is: "**How long should I shuffle?**" There is no strict rule. Some people like to shuffle until they feel ready, or until they sense the deck is well-mixed. Others count a certain number of times (for example, riffle shuffling seven times). You can also shuffle until a card falls out if you believe in "jumping cards" as messages. Ultimately, it is about finding a balance between practicality (ensuring randomness) and the intuitive sense that you have prepared the deck.

11.4.1 When to Stop Shuffling

If you are reading for yourself, you might notice a moment when your mind settles, or the question feels clear. That might be your cue to stop. If you are reading for someone else, you can let them shuffle until they feel done, or you can shuffle while focusing on their question until they say, "Okay, that's enough." Follow your gut and practice until it feels natural.

11.4.2 Jumping or "Pop-Out" Cards

Sometimes, while shuffling, a card (or a few cards) will jump out or fall onto the table. Some readers see this as a special sign—maybe that card wants to be noticed or is particularly relevant. Others pick it up and continue shuffling without giving it extra weight. If you like the idea of "jumping cards," you can set them aside and include them in the reading as an additional message. If that does not resonate with you, no worries—just put them back. It is entirely your choice.

11.5 Handling Reversed Cards (Optional)

We have touched on **reversed cards** in earlier chapters, but we have not focused on how they get reversed in the first place. If you plan to read reversed meanings:

1. **Intentionally flip** some cards in random sections so that half or some portion of the deck is upside down.
2. **Shuffle** as usual, letting the reversed cards stay reversed.
3. **Draw the cards**. If one appears upside down, you read it as reversed.

If you do not want to use reversals, you can keep your deck upright, making sure all cards are facing the same direction. If reversed cards appear by accident, simply turn them right-side up. There is no requirement to read reversed cards—some readers never do.

11.6 Letting Others Shuffle

11.6.1 Client Shuffling

When you read for someone else, you might hand them the deck and let them shuffle while thinking of their question. This can help them feel involved and connected. If you worry about them bending or dropping your cards, give gentle instructions: "Just shuffle in a way that feels comfortable. If you are not used to shuffling, you can do a light overhand or swirl them on the table." Communicating helps them handle your deck carefully.

11.6.2 Reader Shuffling

Some Tarot readers prefer to do all the shuffling themselves. They might ask the client to cut the deck or simply to watch while the reader focuses on the question. Both methods can work. Choose the approach that suits your style. If you sense that the client's physical interaction with the cards is important for their reading, let them shuffle. If you feel more comfortable controlling the deck, do so.

11.7 Cutting the Deck

Cutting the deck usually means splitting it into two or three piles after you finish shuffling, then re-stacking those piles in a new order. Some traditions say to cut with your left hand (symbolizing the subconscious), while others say it does not matter. Cutting the deck is another way to ensure you are not controlling which card is on top.

11.7.1 Client Cutting

If you like, you can ask your client (or yourself, if you are reading for yourself) to cut the deck. This little action can represent them "owning" or "influencing" the final arrangement. Often, the deck is cut once into two piles, then the top pile is placed underneath the bottom pile. Alternatively, the client can create three piles and then reorder them as they wish. Again, there is no absolute rule—experiment and see what feels natural.

11.7.2 No Cutting

Some readers skip cutting entirely. They shuffle thoroughly and then draw the top cards. If that works for you, there is no reason to add an extra step unless you enjoy it. Cutting is a personal preference or a ritual flourish that can add a sense of completeness to the shuffling process.

11.8 Special Shuffle Variations

11.8.1 Single-Card Shuffle

If you are doing a quick one-card draw in the morning, you might do a brief overhand shuffle for a few seconds, thinking about the day ahead. Then you pull the top card or a random card from the middle. This does not require a long, complicated shuffle—just enough to feel you have randomized the deck.

11.8.2 Elemental Shuffles

Some advanced readers create elaborate patterns, like shuffling exactly four times for the four elements (Earth, Air, Fire, Water) or shuffling in cycles of seven for mystical reasons. These are personal or ritual-based choices. If you like numerology or certain symbolic numbers, you can incorporate them into your shuffling. If that seems too fancy, keep it simple.

11.8.3 Clearing Shuffles

After a reading, you might want to do a "clearing shuffle" to ensure the deck is ready for the next question. This can be a quick swirl or overhand shuffle while you briefly focus on releasing the energy of the previous reading. Again, this is optional—some readers just put the deck away after finishing.

11.9 Shuffling and Cultural Traditions

Across different cultures, people have their own card-handling customs. For example, in some places, it is considered polite to let the other person cut the deck. In others, the host or fortune teller always shuffles. If you are reading for someone from a different background (or traveling with your cards), it can be interesting to learn their customs. Doing so can show respect and might open up new ways of seeing the cards.

11.10 Physical Issues and Alternatives

11.10.1 Difficulty with Hands

Some people have arthritis, carpal tunnel, or other hand or wrist issues that make shuffling painful. Overhand shuffling might be easier than riffle shuffling in such cases. The wash method (spreading the cards on the table) can also be gentler, since you do not have to grip the deck tightly.

11.10.2 Using Smaller Decks

If a standard Tarot deck is too large for comfortable shuffling, look for a **pocket-sized** or **travel-sized** deck. These often have the same images, just shrunk down. The smaller cards can be much easier to manage, though the art might be less detailed. It is a trade-off, but it can make shuffling more accessible.

11.10.3 Asking a Helper

If your hands hurt or you cannot shuffle for any reason, you could politely ask someone else to shuffle for you, even if you are the reader. For instance, if you are reading for a friend, you might say, "Would you mind shuffling while I guide the process?" This is a team effort approach—there is no rule that the Tarot reader must do everything alone.

11.11 Setting the Mood While Shuffling

Since shuffling can be a transitional moment, some readers like to set the mood:

- **Soft Music**: Play gentle, instrumental tunes in the background.
- **Aromatherapy**: Light a bit of incense or use a scented candle.
- **Affirmation or Prayer**: Silently say something like, "May this reading bring clarity and insight."

These small touches can enhance the feeling that you are about to do something special. However, you do not need all these things to shuffle well. They are optional additions for those who enjoy a more ritualistic atmosphere.

11.12 Shuffling Exercises to Try

If you are new to Tarot or want to explore different shuffles, here are some mini-exercises:

1. **Mix-and-Match**: Start with an overhand shuffle for 20 seconds, then do a quick riffle shuffle, then spread the cards and swirl them. Notice how each method feels and how it changes your sense of the cards' energy.
2. **Focus Shuffle**: Ask a simple question, like, "What should I keep in mind today?" Shuffle slowly, focusing on that question. Watch your thoughts. Does your mind wander, or can you stay with the question?
3. **Timed Shuffle**: Set a timer for one minute. Shuffle using any method until the timer goes off, then draw the top card. Do you feel that was enough time, too short, or too long?
4. **Reverse Half the Deck**: If you want to practice reversed cards, split the deck in half, flip one half upside down, and then shuffle them together. Spread the cards face-down on a table to see which ones ended up reversed.

11.13 Troubleshooting Shuffling Problems

- **Cards Clumping**: If your cards are new and glossy, they might stick together. You can separate them carefully before the reading. Over time, they will shuffle more easily.
- **Cards Flying Everywhere**: If you shuffle aggressively and cards keep popping out, try slowing down. Or use a gentler style like overhand.
- **Bent or Warped Cards**: Avoid strong bending motions, especially if the deck is large. Store the deck in a safe spot (e.g., in a box or wrapped in a cloth). If the cards warp, you can place them under a heavy book to flatten them.

- **Feeling Awkward**: Beginners often feel clumsy at first, especially if the deck is bigger than standard playing cards. Practice with small chunks of the deck at a time, or do the wash shuffle until you gain confidence.

11.14 Embracing Your Style

There is no single "correct" way to shuffle. Some people do elaborate bridging (creating an arch of cards after riffling), while others do a slow, meditative overhand shuffle. Your style might even change over time or vary depending on the reading. The important thing is to keep the deck random and to feel comfortable. If you develop a personal ritual—like breathing in and out three times before you draw—great! If you prefer to keep it simple and quick, that is also fine.

11.15 Final Thoughts on Shuffling

Shuffling is a humble act, but it plays a big role in Tarot reading. It helps randomize the deck, which is crucial for an honest reading. It also offers a small pause to get centered, clarify your question, and connect with the cards. Whether you choose a quick overhand shuffle or a fancy riffle, treat this process with the care that makes sense to you. Over time, shuffling becomes second nature—a moment of calm before the story of the Tarot unfolds.

Chapter 12: Simple and Advanced Card Spreads

12.1 What Is a Card Spread?

A **card spread** is a pattern or layout in which you place your Tarot cards during a reading. Each position in a spread has a specific meaning or role. For example, in a three-card spread, one position might represent the past, another the present, and another the future. By placing a card in each spot, you give context to how each card's message fits into your overall question or situation.

Spreads help you organize your reading. Instead of drawing a bunch of random cards and guessing how they fit together, you have a structured map. The spread tells you, "This card shows your challenge, that card shows your hidden strengths, and that card shows the likely outcome," or whatever the positions are designated to represent.

12.2 Why Use Spreads?

12.2.1 Clarity and Focus

A spread guides you so you do not get lost in too many possibilities. When you draw multiple cards at once, it can be overwhelming. A spread breaks the reading into smaller pieces. You can say, "Let me examine the card in the position for obstacles," then move on to the card in the position for advice, etc. This structure can make the reading more coherent.

12.2.2 Answering Specific Questions

Different spreads are suited to different types of questions. If you want a quick overview of a situation, a three-card spread might be enough. If you want a deep dive into your love life, you might pick a relationship spread with positions for each partner's feelings and possible outcomes. Tailoring the spread to your question can yield more precise insights.

12.2.3 Tradition and Creativity

Some spreads have been around for centuries (like the Celtic Cross). Others are newly invented by modern readers. You can follow well-known patterns or create your own. Learning different spreads can expand your Tarot toolkit, letting you pick the right layout for each reading.

12.3 Getting Started: Simple Spreads

12.3.1 One-Card Draw

The **one-card draw** is the simplest "spread." In fact, it is just a single card. It can be great for daily reflections or quick guidance. You shuffle, pull one card, and ask, "What do I need to know right now?" or "What is the main theme for today?" Then you interpret the card. This is easy and less intimidating than large spreads.

Pros:

- Quick and direct.
- Good for everyday use.
- Helps you focus on one clear message.

Cons:

- Provides limited detail.
- Might not address complex questions.

12.3.2 Three-Card Spread

One of the most popular basic spreads is the **three-card spread**. It is versatile because you can assign many possible meanings to the three positions. Common patterns include:

1. **Past – Present – Future**
2. **Situation – Advice – Outcome**
3. **You – The Other Person – Relationship Energy**
4. **Mind – Body – Spirit**
5. **Option A – Option B – What to Consider** (for decision-making)

By deciding in advance what the three positions represent, you create a neat framework. It is simple enough not to overwhelm a beginner, yet flexible enough to explore many topics.

12.3.3 Yes/No Spreads (With Caution)

Some people want a yes/no answer. The Tarot is not always best for yes/no questions, because it speaks in symbols and nuances rather than plain "yes" or "no." However, if you must, you can use a one-card or three-card method:

- For a **one-card yes/no**, you might decide that upright means "yes" and reversed means "no," or black suits (Swords, Wands) mean "no" and red suits (Cups, Pentacles) mean "yes" in certain decks that color-code.
- For a **three-card yes/no**, you might say 2 or more upright cards = yes, else no.

Be aware that this approach can be oversimplified, since Tarot usually deals with deeper advice than just "yes" or "no."

12.4 Intermediate Spreads

12.4.1 The Celtic Cross

The **Celtic Cross** is a classic. It is an old spread that many beginners learn eventually. It uses ten cards, placed in a specific pattern. The layout often looks like this:

```
       5      10
   3   1/2    6
       4      9
              8
              7
```

- **Card 1**: The present situation or the person's core position.
- **Card 2**: The crossing card—an obstacle or factor affecting the situation.
- **Card 3**: The foundation or the cause behind it all.
- **Card 4**: The recent past.
- **Card 5**: What is on the person's mind or best outcome.
- **Card 6**: The near future.
- **Card 7**: The person's attitude or how they see themselves.
- **Card 8**: External influences or how others see the situation.
- **Card 9**: Hopes and fears.
- **Card 10**: The likely outcome if things continue as they are.

There are variations on these position names, but the idea is to get a comprehensive view. The Celtic Cross can be powerful and in-depth, but it is also a lot of information. Beginners might find it a bit overwhelming at first. With practice, though, it becomes a staple spread that can address almost any question.

Tips for the Celtic Cross:

- Start by interpreting Card 1 and Card 2 together to see the core conflict or issue.
- Move in sequence, linking each card's meaning to the story forming in the layout.
- Pay special attention to Card 10 (the outcome), but remember that free will can change that result.

12.4.2 The Horseshoe Spread

The **Horseshoe Spread** typically uses seven cards arranged in a curve or line that resembles a horseshoe. Positions might be:

1. **Past**
2. **Present**
3. **Hidden influences**
4. **Advice**
5. **Obstacles**
6. **External resources**
7. **Probable outcome**

You can modify these positions to suit your question. The horseshoe shape helps you visually see how the story moves from left (past) to right (future outcome). This spread gives a bit more depth than a three-card reading but is not as large as the Celtic Cross.

12.4.3 Relationship Spread (5 or 7 Cards)

For relationship questions—romantic or otherwise—there are many possible layouts. A simple 5-card relationship spread might look like this:

1. **You** (your feelings, mindset)
2. **Your Partner** (their feelings, mindset)

3. **Core Issue** (the main dynamic between you)
4. **Advice or Guidance** (what can help the relationship)
5. **Possible Outcome** (if things continue as they are)

A 7-card version could add positions for "Past," "Present," "Future," or "What needs healing" and "What can be celebrated." The idea is to explore each partner's perspective and see what the cards say about the connection.

12.5 Advanced Spreads

12.5.1 The Astrological Spread (12 Houses)

Some readers use a **12-house astrological spread**, laying 12 cards in a circle—each representing a house of the zodiac (e.g., 1st house = identity, 2nd = finances, 3rd = communication, etc.). This spread can give an in-depth look at various life areas, from relationships to career, from home life to spirituality. It is quite detailed and might take a long time to interpret. You do not need to be an astrology expert to try it, but basic familiarity helps.

12.5.2 Year Ahead Spread

A **year ahead spread** is often done around birthdays or New Year's. You lay out 12 or 13 cards—one card per month plus maybe one overall theme card. Each card describes the energy or events you might face that month. You can do this in a circle or in a row. Some folks keep track of each monthly card in a journal and review it as time passes.

12.5.3 Creating Your Own Spread

Once you are comfortable with standard layouts, try inventing a spread tailored to your question. For example, if you want to look at a creative project, you could design positions like:

1. **Initial Inspiration**
2. **Challenges**
3. **Resources**
4. **Next Step**
5. **Outcome**

You can add more positions if needed. Customize the shape—maybe a star or a spiral. Let your imagination guide you. This personal approach can be very satisfying because it aligns perfectly with your question.

12.6 How to Approach a Spread

12.6.1 Step-by-Step Reading

When you lay out multiple cards, it helps to have a **system**. For instance:

1. **State the question** clearly.
2. **Shuffle and lay out** the cards in the chosen spread.
3. **Identify each position** (e.g., "This is the Advice card," "This is the Outcome card").
4. **Interpret each card** one by one, keeping in mind the position meaning.
5. **Look for links** between the cards. Do you see repeating symbols or suits?
6. **Summarize the overall message**. Bring the parts together into a cohesive story.

Taking notes can help you remember your impressions. Some people snap a photo of the layout so they can revisit it later.

12.6.2 Reading Card Interactions

In a spread, cards do not stand alone. A card in the "obstacle" position might link with a card in the "advice" position. For example, if you have the **Five of Wands** (conflict) in obstacles and the **Temperance** card in advice, that might suggest the conflict is a result of people not blending their energies well, and Temperance is urging cooperation and balance.

Look for **suits** or **numbers** that repeat. If you see many swords, communication or mental stress might be key. If you see multiple tens, you might be at a point of completion in various aspects of your life. Patterns help you see the big picture.

12.6.3 Major vs. Minor Arcana Emphasis

Notice whether you have many **Major Arcana** cards in a spread. That can indicate deep or significant changes. If your reading is mostly **Minor Arcana**, it might be more about day-to-day or practical concerns. The presence of Court Cards could highlight people or personality traits that are relevant to the question.

12.7 Interpreting Specific Positions

12.7.1 Past, Present, Future

A common trio is "Past, Present, Future." The Past card can show what led to the current situation or what you have learned. The Present card indicates the energy now or your current influences. The Future card suggests a possible outcome or direction if you stay on this path. This is a straightforward way to see a timeline. Just remember that the future is never set in stone—Tarot offers possibilities, not certainties.

12.7.2 Hopes and Fears

In spreads like the Celtic Cross, one position is often labeled **Hopes/Fears**. This can be tricky because what we hope for can also be what we fear. For instance, you may hope for a promotion but fear the responsibilities that come with it. When you see the card in this spot, consider both sides. If the card is The Tower, maybe you hope for a big change but also fear the chaos it might bring.

12.7.3 Advice or Guidance

If a spread has an **Advice** position, that card is crucial. It often tells you what attitude or action might help most. For example, if you draw the **Queen of Cups** in Advice, you might need a compassionate, empathetic approach. If you draw the **Knight of Swords**, perhaps you should speak up boldly or move quickly. This position can be your "takeaway" for practical steps forward.

12.8 Practical Tips for Spreads

12.8.1 Not Every Spread Needs All 78 Cards

Spreads come in all sizes. Some use 3 cards, some use 10, some use 24, and so on. Start small. If you try to read 15 cards but are still learning, you might feel overwhelmed. It is better to do a smaller spread and interpret each card carefully than to do a huge spread and get lost.

12.8.2 Write Down the Positions

If you are learning a new spread, **write down** what each position stands for before you lay out the cards. It is easy to forget which position is which if you are new or if the spread is large. Having a note in front of you—like "Card 1: Situation, Card 2: Challenge, Card 3: Root Cause, etc."—will keep you on track.

12.8.3 Adapting Spreads

Feel free to adjust a spread's positions if something does not resonate. For instance, if you are using the Horseshoe Spread but do not like a certain position, rename it or replace it with something more relevant. Tarot is flexible, and spreads are guidelines, not strict laws.

12.8.4 Practice on Real Questions

Practicing with real situations—your own or your friends'—helps you see how spreads work in actual readings. Doing a Celtic Cross just for the sake of practice is okay, but applying it to a real-life problem is more enlightening. You will notice how the cards speak to the question in unique ways.

12.9 Sample Spread Walkthrough

Let us try a quick example with a simple 5-card spread for a career question. We define the positions:

1. **Current Job Situation**
2. **Obstacle/Challenge**
3. **Hidden Strength**
4. **Advice for Growth**
5. **Likely Outcome**

Imagine these cards come up:

1. **Two of Pentacles** (Current Job)
2. **Five of Wands** (Obstacle)
3. **Magician** (Hidden Strength)

4. **Knight of Pentacles** (Advice)
5. **Ten of Cups** (Likely Outcome)
- **Two of Pentacles** at Current Job: Suggests juggling multiple tasks, trying to keep balance.
- **Five of Wands** at Obstacle: Points to competition or conflict at work, maybe coworkers not cooperating.
- **Magician** at Hidden Strength: You have the skill set and tools to handle this. You can manifest solutions if you believe in your abilities.
- **Knight of Pentacles** at Advice: Be consistent, patient, methodical. Do not rush. Focus on quality and persistence.
- **Ten of Cups** at Likely Outcome: Promises a fulfilling result if you follow through. Harmony can be achieved. Possibly a stable, happy workplace or personal sense of accomplishment.

From these five cards, you can weave a story: "You are busy juggling tasks (Two of Pentacles) amidst workplace competition (Five of Wands). However, you secretly have all the tools you need (Magician). The advice is to stay diligent and patient (Knight of Pentacles), and you can find genuine satisfaction (Ten of Cups)." That is a simple example of how a structured spread can clarify your reading.

12.10 Handling Multiple Questions

12.10.1 One Spread per Question

Often, you might do one spread per main question. If you have a second question, you can shuffle and lay out new cards. Some people try to cram multiple questions into a single spread, which can be confusing. It is usually better to focus on one question at a time, especially if the spread is already large.

12.10.2 Follow-Up Spreads

If, after reading your first spread, you need more detail on a particular aspect, you can do a smaller follow-up spread. For example, if the Celtic Cross reveals a big emphasis on your finances, you might do a quick 3-card spread specifically about finances to clarify that part of the message.

12.11 Reversals in Spreads

If you read reversed cards, you can apply those interpretations in any spread. A reversed card in the "Advice" position might mean a blocked or delayed form of advice, or it could be urging you to release something. As always, reversed interpretations depend on how you see reversed meanings—some see them as the opposite, others see them as a challenge or internal energy. The spread position can guide you on how to read the reversal.

12.12 Timing in Spreads

12.12.1 "When Will This Happen?"

Tarot is not always great at giving exact dates. Some readers try to assign time frames to suits (e.g., Wands for days, Swords for weeks, Cups for months, Pentacles for years), or they look at the seasons. Others do not focus on timing at all, emphasizing that Tarot shows potential energies rather than a fixed schedule. If you want to explore timing, you can create a spread with a position labeled "Time Frame," but be flexible in interpretation.

12.12.2 Checking Progress Over Time

Some readers revisit a spread weeks later to see if events unfolded as suggested. This can help you learn the deck's "language" for timing. If you notice that a certain card reliably shows events within a month or so, that might be how the Tarot communicates time to you. Keep a journal to track these patterns.

12.13 Group Readings and Spreads

12.13.1 Collective Spreads

If you are reading for a group—like friends at a gathering—you might do a single spread for everyone to see. Each position could represent a group dynamic, or you could interpret how each card applies to each person. That can be fun but also complicated. Make sure everyone understands that the reading might be more general, and personal details might not be as precise.

12.13.2 Partner or Team Spreads

You can design a spread for two people working together on a project, with positions like "Person A's viewpoint," "Person B's viewpoint," "Shared goal," "Challenges," "How to collaborate," "Potential outcome." This approach can also work for teams of three or more, though you need enough positions to cover each person. For large groups, short readings or single-card pulls are often simpler.

12.14 Trusting Your Instinct

Sometimes, a card's position in the spread might not match the typical textbook meaning. Trust your instinct. For example, if the

Devil appears in the "Challenge" position, you might interpret it as obsession or feeling trapped. If that same card appears in the "Advice" position, it might indicate you need to confront your own fears or break free from limiting beliefs. Let the combination of the card's traditional meaning, the position label, and your intuitive sense guide your reading.

12.15 When a Spread Feels Confusing

It is normal to feel confused occasionally. Maybe you draw contradictory cards. Or you do not see how the outcome card relates to the rest. Here are some strategies:

1. **Re-check the position meanings**: Are you mixing them up?
2. **Look for card relationships**: Do two cards clash, or do they secretly complement each other?
3. **Pull a clarifier card**: Some readers draw an extra card to clarify a puzzling card or position.
4. **Journal your thoughts**: Sometimes writing it down helps you see a pattern.
5. **Take a break**: If you are stuck, step away for a bit and come back with fresh eyes.

12.16 Creating a Reading Flow

A good Tarot reading flow might look like this:

1. **Shuffle** (Chapter 11 taught you how) while focusing on the question.
2. **Pick or create a spread** suitable for the question (simple, intermediate, or advanced).
3. **Lay out the cards** in the chosen pattern, naming each position.
4. **Interpret** card by card, noting position context.

5. **Link** the cards to form a coherent narrative.
6. **Give advice or summary** that helps the question-asker (yourself or someone else) find clarity or direction.
7. **Close** the reading, optionally shuffling again to clear the deck.

This framework ensures you do not miss any key step and that you deliver a reading that feels complete.

12.17 Practice: Designing Your Own Spread

Try creating a personal spread for something you care about. Let us say you want a spread about "Moving to a New Home." You could set up:

1. **Current Living Situation** (card 1)
2. **What I Desire in a New Home** (card 2)
3. **Obstacles to Moving** (card 3)
4. **Help or Resources** (card 4)
5. **Action Steps** (card 5)
6. **Likely Outcome of the Move** (card 6)

Place the cards in a layout that feels good—maybe a circle or a line. Once you draw, interpret each position. Notice how creating a custom spread can tailor the reading precisely to your question.

Chapter 13: Reading the Symbols and Images

13.1 Why Symbols Matter in Tarot

When you look at a Tarot card, you see more than just a picture. You see a collection of symbols and images that each carry meaning. These symbols often tap into our subconscious minds. For example, a sun can suggest hope or clarity, while a path might represent a journey or choice. Even colors like red or blue can spark emotions or ideas. By learning to read these symbols and images carefully, you can unlock deeper insights from each card.

Tarot's power partly comes from these visual cues. They can trigger memories, feelings, or sudden "aha!" moments. You might see a stream of water in a card and think of cleansing or flow, or you might see a crown and think of authority or leadership. Over centuries, decks have used imagery tied to universal human experiences. That is why people from many cultures can find value in Tarot—it speaks a symbolic language that goes beyond words.

13.2 Approaching Symbols: A Step-by-Step Method

13.2.1 First Impressions

When you first flip a card, **pause and look** at it. Notice the main figure or object. Ask yourself: "What does my eye go to right away?" Sometimes, it might be a person's face. Other times, you might notice a tree in the background or a color that pops out. This first impression can be vital. It often holds the emotional energy that the card carries for you at that moment.

13.2.2 Break Down the Elements

Next, try to identify key parts of the image:

- **People or figures**: What are they doing? How do they look (happy, sad, determined, relaxed)?
- **Animals or creatures**: Are there lions, dogs, birds? Animals often symbolize traits like loyalty (dogs), courage (lions), or insight (owls).
- **Objects**: Are there swords, cups, or flowers? Which object stands out?
- **Setting**: Is it indoors or outdoors? Are there mountains, rivers, or buildings?
- **Colors**: Which colors dominate? Bright yellow might suggest optimism, while gray skies might suggest doubt.

Try listing each noticeable element. You might say, "Person wearing a red robe, holding a cup, with a fish popping out of it. Water in the background." Breaking it down helps you see details you might miss if you only glance quickly.

13.2.3 Interpret Each Element

Once you have identified the elements, think about **why** they might be there. A fish might relate to creativity or surprise, water might symbolize emotions, and a red robe might hint at passion or energy. If you notice a mountain, consider what it means in your personal context—maybe a challenge or a high goal.

Tarot creators often place these items intentionally. Even small details like a tiny flower can carry significance. However, do not feel you must memorize every possible meaning. Instead, let your mind associate freely and see what resonates. Sometimes, your own personal experiences give these symbols a unique meaning.

13.2.4 Weave It Together

Finally, form a story or concept that brings these elements together. For example, if you see a person standing by a river under a sunny sky, holding a wand, you might say: "This card suggests taking creative action (wand) in a time of emotional flow (river) with optimism (sun)." This weaving is where the magic of Tarot often happens. You start seeing how the elements combine to speak about your situation.

13.3 Common Tarot Symbols and Their Meanings

While every deck can differ, many symbols recur across decks. Below are some widespread ones, along with general interpretations. Remember, these are not strict definitions. Your personal connection might add or change the meaning.

13.3.1 The Sun

- **Likely Meaning**: Positivity, clarity, warmth, success.
- **When You See It**: The card might encourage hope or a bright outlook. It often signals good news or a clear path forward.

13.3.2 The Moon

- **Likely Meaning**: Mystery, intuition, the subconscious, sometimes confusion.
- **When You See It**: The card might suggest you are not seeing everything clearly, or that you should trust your instincts.

13.3.3 Stars

- **Likely Meaning**: Guidance, inspiration, hope, faith in the future.
- **When You See It**: Look for a sense of being guided by a higher ideal or dream. It may also suggest healing and calm.

13.3.4 Water / Rivers / Oceans

- **Likely Meaning**: Emotions, intuition, fluidity, depth.
- **When You See It**: Emphasizes feeling, empathy, or a need to "go with the flow." Could also signal emotional healing or a cleansing stage.

13.3.5 Mountains

- **Likely Meaning**: Challenges, aspirations, obstacles to climb, high achievements.
- **When You See It**: You might face a test that requires perseverance, or you might be aiming for a lofty goal.

13.3.6 Paths or Roads

- **Likely Meaning**: Choices, direction, journey, the next step.
- **When You See It**: Often hints at needing to decide which way to go or acknowledging a journey you are on.

13.3.7 Animals (Dogs, Lions, Birds, etc.)

- **Dogs**: Loyalty, friendship, guidance, protection.
- **Lions**: Courage, power, raw energy.
- **Birds**: Freedom, higher perspective, messages from above.
- **Fish**: Creativity, abundance, hidden insights (especially in Cups cards).

13.3.8 Colors

- **Red**: Passion, energy, sometimes anger or strong drive.
- **Blue**: Calm, emotion, introspection.
- **Yellow**: Optimism, clarity, intellect.
- **Green**: Growth, nature, healing.
- **Black**: Mystery, the unknown, sometimes fear or hidden truths.
- **White**: Purity, innocence, clarity of thought.

By recognizing these common symbols, you can quickly get a sense of the card's mood. But always stay open to how you personally react to them. If you had a beloved black cat growing up, black might feel comforting rather than mysterious!

13.4 The Importance of Context

13.4.1 Card Combinations

A single symbol can shift meaning depending on the other symbols in the card. For example, a lion in one card might look gentle, while in another card it is roaring aggressively. The environment changes the interpretation. In a spread, too, the presence of certain cards can alter how you see a symbol. For instance, if The Tower appears next to a peaceful nature scene, you might interpret the scene as a calm after a sudden shake-up.

13.4.2 Suit and Number

If you are reading the Minor Arcana, remember that **suit** (Cups, Pentacles, Swords, Wands) and the **number** (Ace to 10) also shape the message. The symbols of water might mean something slightly different in the suit of Cups (which is already about emotions) than in the suit of Swords (which is usually about thoughts). Also, a 2 might symbolize partnership, while a 10 might mean completion or the final stage.

13.4.3 Major Arcana vs. Minor Arcana Imagery

Major Arcana cards tend to have bigger, more archetypal symbols—like The Lovers, The Sun, Death, or The Empress. These often relate to life-changing themes. Minor Arcana symbols are sometimes more everyday or practical. When you see a strong symbol in a Major Arcana card, it might carry more weight in your reading.

13.5 Using Symbolism with Different Decks

13.5.1 Rider-Waite-Smith Style

The **Rider-Waite-Smith** (RWS) deck is one of the most common. It is rich in symbols—like the sunflowers in The Sun card or the pillars in The High Priestess. Many modern decks base their images and symbols on RWS, so if you learn RWS symbols, you can often adapt them to other decks.

13.5.2 Themed Decks

Some decks focus on specific themes—cats, dragons, fairies, or certain mythologies. The symbols might change accordingly. A cat-themed deck might use different cat poses or colors to convey messages. A dragon-themed deck might use scales, claws, or flames as core symbols. While the foundation is similar, you need to see how the artist reinterprets classic Tarot images in that theme.

13.5.3 Minimalist Decks

Some decks are very simple, showing only the suit symbols or abstract shapes. In those decks, color, shape, and layout become even more important. If the deck has a limited palette or few details, you might rely more on the known meaning of the card name (like "8 of Wands") or your own intuition. You can still look for small hints—like one wand being angled differently—but the symbolism might be subtler.

13.6 Personal Symbols and Cultural Influences

13.6.1 Personal Associations

Your life experiences shape how you read symbols. If your grandmother always wore a purple scarf and you see purple in a card, you might instantly think of her wisdom. Another person might see purple as regal or spiritual. Neither is wrong. Personal associations can add layers of meaning to your readings. That is part of what makes Tarot so unique for each reader.

13.6.2 Cultural Meanings

Symbols also vary across cultures. For instance, white can mean purity in some cultures but mourning in others. A dragon might be evil in one mythology but benevolent in another. If you come from or resonate with a certain cultural background, that might shift how you interpret certain images. A deck created in another part of the world could show symbols you have never encountered before. Keep an open mind and do some research if needed. Or, trust your instincts and let the symbol speak to you personally.

13.7 Techniques to Deepen Symbolic Understanding

13.7.1 Journaling

A great way to learn Tarot symbols is to **journal**. Pick one card. Write down every symbol you see. Then write a quick interpretation of each symbol. You might add how that symbol relates to your current question or mood. Revisit your notes later to see if your understanding evolves. Over time, you will build a personal dictionary of Tarot symbols.

13.7.2 Visualization

Another technique is **visualization**. Close your eyes and imagine stepping into the card. If you see a river, imagine dipping your hand in the water. How does it feel? If there is a mountain, imagine climbing it or looking at the view from the top. This daydream-like approach can help you sense what the symbols represent on a deeper, emotional level.

13.7.3 Comparing Decks

If you own more than one deck, compare how they depict the same card. For example, look at The Lovers in the Rider-Waite-Smith deck and The Lovers in a cat-themed deck. Notice what is the same (a theme of union or choice) and what is different (maybe the cat deck shows two cats under a big heart). By observing these differences, you gain a broader sense of what is truly central to that card's symbolism and how artists adapt it.

13.8 Symbolic "Clues" in a Reading

13.8.1 Repetitions

If you lay out several cards and see repeated symbols—like multiple suns, repeated water scenes, or many green backdrops—pay attention. That repetition could be the deck's way of emphasizing a theme. For instance, if you see lots of water, it might be a sign you need to handle emotional or intuitive matters.

13.8.2 Contrasts

Sometimes a card with bright colors sits beside a card with dark, stormy imagery. This contrast might highlight a conflict or a balance you need. One card might represent your fears, while the other represents a path to relief. Contrasts can draw your attention to polarities—like light/dark, calm/chaos, or personal freedom/commitment.

13.8.3 Body Language

In cards that show people, pay attention to their **body language**. Are they reaching out, turning away, pointing at something? A figure who looks at a certain object might direct you to examine that symbol more closely. A figure with arms raised might suggest triumph or calling upon higher powers. Body language can be as telling as an actual word bubble in a comic.

13.9 Pitfalls in Symbol Reading

13.9.1 Overthinking

It is possible to overanalyze. If you stare too long at every tiny detail, you might lose the overall message. Sometimes a small symbol is just

part of the artwork style or decorative filler. You have to use balance.
Start with the big picture, then notice the key details that stand out.
Do not force meaning onto every dot or line if it does not feel
relevant.

13.9.2 Relying Solely on Books

Guidebooks or reference books can help you learn symbols, but do
not rely on them so much that you ignore your own impressions. If a
book says a red rose always means passion, but you feel it means
devotion or memory, trust your reaction. Books offer general
insights, but your personal connection matters too.

13.9.3 Ignoring Context

Symbols do not exist in isolation. Always check the card's entire
scene, the spread position, and your question. If you ignore these
factors, you might twist a symbol's meaning into something it is not.
For instance, a snake can be cunning in one context but healing (like
the medical caduceus) in another.

13.10 Examples of Symbolic Interpretation

13.10.1 Example 1: The Hermit (Major Arcana)

- **Imagery**: A robed figure holding a lantern, often standing on a mountain.
- **Symbols**:
    - Lantern: Illumination, inner light, guiding wisdom.
    - Mountain: Solitude, challenge, spiritual peak.
    - Hooded robe: Secrecy, introspection, detachment from the world.
- **Interpretation**: Encourages seeking knowledge in quiet places, reflecting on your path, or guiding others with what

you have learned. The lantern can mean shining truth on hidden areas of your life.

13.10.2 Example 2: Three of Swords (Minor Arcana)

- **Imagery**: A heart pierced by three swords, often with a stormy background.
- **Symbols**:
    - Heart: Love, emotions, core of feelings.
    - Swords: Conflict, mental strife, sharp truths.
    - Rain/Clouds: Sadness, emotional release, cleansing tears.
- **Interpretation**: Signifies heartbreak, betrayal, sorrow, or emotional pain. The storm can suggest tears and grief, but also that storms eventually pass. The heart's presence indicates the wound is emotional at its core. This card might nudge you to face a painful truth before you can heal.

13.10.3 Example 3: Six of Wands (Minor Arcana)

- **Imagery**: A rider on a horse, often holding a wand with a wreath, with a cheering crowd.
- **Symbols**:
    - Horse: Movement forward, journey, progress.
    - Wreath: Victory, achievement, celebration.
    - Crowd: Public recognition, support from others.
- **Interpretation**: Suggests success, acknowledgment, or winning a challenge. The wand is about energy and passion, so this card can mean you are being celebrated for your efforts. The crowd might show that success is not just private but also recognized publicly.

These examples show how symbols combine to tell a story. Notice the difference in mood and theme. Each card has a blend of objects, colors, and atmosphere that shapes its message.

13.11 Making Symbol Reading a Habit

13.11.1 Daily Card Observation

Try drawing a card each morning and quickly note its main symbols. If you see a sunrise in the card, think about how a new day might bring fresh starts for you. If you see a scale (as in Justice), reflect on your need for balance that day. Even a few minutes of symbolic awareness can keep your intuition sharp.

13.11.2 Symbol Scavenger Hunt

Pick a particular symbol—like "flowers"—and look for it in various cards. Some decks have flowers in many cards. Notice which types appear: roses, lilies, sunflowers, daisies? Each might represent love, purity, vitality, innocence. By zooming in on a single symbol across different cards, you see how the deck uses that image to convey different angles.

13.11.3 Personal Symbol Glossary

You can create a small notebook or digital file listing symbols alphabetically. For instance:

- **Bird** – Freedoms, messages, vantage points, or journeys.
- **Bridge** – Transition, crossing from one phase to another, connecting two areas.
- **Circle** – Wholeness, unity, cycles, something that comes around again.

Each time you encounter a new or interesting symbol, add your personal notes. Over time, you will build a resource that is unique to your style and experiences.

Chapter 14: Using Intuition and Inner Senses

14.1 What Is Intuition?

Intuition is that **inner knowing** or gut feeling that does not come from logical thinking alone. Sometimes, you might say, "I just knew I should take that job," or, "I had a hunch my friend was upset." This knowing can feel subtle or sudden. In Tarot reading, intuition helps you see beyond written card meanings and symbolic analysis. It weaves together your feelings, experiences, and subconscious signals, guiding you to an interpretation that resonates deeply.

You might wonder, "Is intuition the same as psychic power?" Not exactly. While some people use the term "psychic," others see intuition as a natural human sense. It is like an inner sense that picks up on subtle cues—body language, emotional tone, personal memories—before your logical mind does. When you use Tarot, your intuition can help you notice meaningful connections among the cards, or sense when a particular interpretation feels "right" or "off."

14.2 Why Intuition Is Important in Tarot

14.2.1 Beyond Book Definitions

Tarot guidebooks are helpful, but they cannot cover every life context or emotional nuance. Suppose you see the Five of Pentacles, which often means financial struggle or feeling excluded. However, your intuition might say, "In this reading, it is not about money, but about self-confidence." That intuitive leap may come from the person's posture in the card, or your gut sense that the question is really about self-worth. Intuition fills gaps that standardized meanings cannot.

14.2.2 Personal Connections

Everyone's life story is unique. A certain card might remind you of a specific memory or dream. When that card appears, your intuition might nudge you, "Remember that time you overcame a similar challenge." This personal link can shed light on how to interpret the card for your current situation. The intuitive insight often feels tailor-made for you, something no generic definition could predict.

14.2.3 Heightened Sensitivity

Tarot readings can touch emotional or spiritual levels. By engaging your intuition, you become more sensitive to feelings, subtle shifts in mood, or unspoken concerns. If you are reading for someone else, your intuition might pick up that they are anxious or holding back important details. This can guide you to ask gentle questions or focus on certain cards that resonate with their hidden worries.

14.3 Cultivating Intuition

Some people think intuition is a magical gift you either have or do not have. But in reality, you can **develop** your intuitive abilities with practice. Here are ways to do it:

14.3.1 Quiet the Mind

In daily life, our minds are busy with tasks, worries, and distractions. Intuition often speaks in a quieter voice. When you slow down and clear some mental clutter, you create space for that inner whisper. **Meditation** is one common technique: sit or lie down, breathe slowly, and gently let go of racing thoughts. Even a few minutes a day can help you become more receptive to subtle impressions.

14.3.2 Daily Tarot Draw with Reflection

Pull a single card each morning and ask, "How might this card relate to my day?" Then, as the day unfolds, notice if anything lines up with that card's energy. At night, reflect on whether your initial feeling was accurate. This exercise trains your intuition to link the card's imagery with real-life experiences in a personal, immediate way.

14.3.3 Trust Small Hunches

Throughout the day, notice small hunches—like which route to drive, or when to check in on a friend. Make a mental note of how often these hunches turn out to be right. By recognizing that your intuition does guide you in everyday life, you build confidence. Over time, you trust it more during Tarot readings.

14.3.4 Freewriting or Journaling

After drawing a card, **freewrite** for five minutes about what you sense. Write in a stream-of-consciousness style, not worrying about grammar or structure. Let your pen flow with any images, words, or feelings that pop up. This can bypass your overthinking mind and let intuitive impressions surface.

14.4 Balancing Logic and Intuition

While intuition is powerful, **logic** and rational thought also matter. Good Tarot reading often blends both. For example:

- **Logical Side**: You know from your studies that the Death card often symbolizes transformation rather than literal death.
- **Intuitive Side**: You feel that in this reading, it specifically points to ending a toxic friendship or job situation.

You do not ignore the standard meaning, but you do not rely on it blindly either. Instead, you let your intuition refine and shape the meaning to fit the context of the question. This balance ensures you stay grounded and do not float away on random feelings, but also remain open to deeper insights that standard definitions might miss.

14.5 Techniques for Intuitive Tarot Reading

14.5.1 The Quick Glance Method

When you flip a card, glance at it briefly, then close your eyes. Ask yourself, "What do I remember? How does it make me feel?" This prevents you from obsessing over every detail and allows your subconscious to highlight what stands out. If you recall a bright color or a certain object, that might be the intuitive clue you need.

14.5.2 Body Sensations

Pay attention to your **body**. Sometimes, a card might make you feel a knot in your stomach (signaling worry or caution), or a warmth in your chest (signaling love or relief). This is sometimes called "clairsentience" or "clear feeling." Trust these physical signals as part of your reading. For instance, if you get a tense feeling when you see The Devil card, maybe the reading is about being trapped in fear or addiction. If you feel calm with The Star, it might indicate hope and serenity.

14.5.3 Emotional Shift

Notice any emotional change. If you suddenly feel sad, excited, or uneasy, that might be your intuition reacting to the card's message. You can also ask, "Why am I feeling this way?" Maybe you sense the reading is pointing to unresolved grief or an upcoming burst of inspiration. Emotions can be a powerful channel for intuitive hits.

14.5.4 Visual Imagery or Daydreams

While looking at the card, let your mind wander into an **inner daydream**. Imagine you are walking into the scene. What do you hear, smell, or feel? Who else is there? This guided imagery can spark details that logic alone might miss. For example, if you daydream that you talk to The Hermit and he warns you to slow down, that might be your intuition telling you to take a step back in real life.

14.5.5 Dialogue with the Card

Another fun technique is to imagine you can **talk** to the figure on the card. Ask questions: "What do you want me to know? Why are you holding that lamp? Where are we going?" Let answers bubble up from within. This might feel like make-believe, but it can unlock genuine insights. You are giving your intuition a playful space to speak.

14.6 Signs of Authentic Intuition

One challenge is distinguishing real intuitive insight from wishful thinking or fear-based guesswork. Here are some hints that you are tapping genuine intuition:

- **Calm Certainty**: Often, intuition arrives without frantic energy. It feels steady, even if it is surprising.
- **Sudden Clarity**: You might feel a click of understanding or see a clear mental image.
- **Simplicity**: Intuition can be straightforward, not always wrapped in complex justifications.
- **Resonance**: You sense the message resonates with a deeper part of you. You might think, "Yes, that's right," even if it is unexpected.

14.7 Working Through Doubts

14.7.1 Fear of Being Wrong

It is normal to worry about making a wrong guess. But remember, Tarot readings are interpretive. Even experienced readers sometimes question their insights. The best approach is to say, "Here is what I feel strongly," while being open to correction or new information. Over time, you will see patterns of what resonates most often.

14.7.2 Trying Too Hard to "Be Psychic"

Chasing dramatic psychic feats can cloud your intuitive process. You might over-embellish or force fancy visions. True intuition often arises gently. If you find yourself straining to see wild visions, take a breath and return to basics—look at the card, check your emotions, and see what subtle thoughts come up.

14.7.3 External Validation

Sometimes, you want external proof that your intuition is correct. In a reading for someone else, their feedback might confirm your insights. But do not get hooked on constant approval. Trust-building is an internal process. Over-focusing on other people's reactions can stifle your natural flow. Accept that sometimes your reading might not make sense immediately to the other person, or it might require time to unfold.

14.8 Combining Intuition with Symbol Knowledge

14.8.1 Symbol as a Doorway

In Chapter 13, we learned about symbols. You can use these as "doorways" to let your intuition walk through. For instance, if you see a snake symbol (common in some cards), you know from a book that a snake can mean rebirth or danger. Now let your intuition weigh in: does it feel more like growth this time, or a risky trap? Does a memory or feeling bubble up? Symbol knowledge sets the stage; intuition decides how it plays in your scenario.

14.8.2 Rewriting Symbol Meanings

Over time, your intuition might update how you see certain symbols. For example, you once read that a white flower means purity. But your personal experience might link white flowers with mourning after losing a loved one. Honor that shift. Tarot is dynamic, and your interpretive lens can evolve as you do. This is a sign of growth, not inconsistency.

14.9 Exercises to Boost Intuitive Reading

14.9.1 Card Storytelling

Take a random card from your deck. Spend five minutes inventing a short **story**. Describe the character, the setting, and a conflict they face. Do not worry if it relates to standard card meanings. Just create a narrative. Then reflect: does this story mirror anything in your life? Did certain themes pop out unexpectedly? This can spark intuitive connections that reveal how the card relates to you.

14.9.2 Musical Interpretation

Play a piece of instrumental music with no lyrics. Pull one card. Look at it while the music plays. Notice how the card's mood changes with the rhythm or melody. If the music is haunting, does that make the card feel more ominous or emotional? If the music is joyful, does the card seem more optimistic? This can help you sense different layers of emotion in a single image, building intuition about tone and atmosphere.

14.9.3 Pair Reading with a Friend

If you have a friend who is also learning Tarot, do a reading for each other. After you lay out the cards, say what you sense intuitively. Then ask your friend if anything resonates with them. Encourage them to share their own intuitive take. Watching someone else's process can give you new ideas for how to tune into your own inner sense. This mutual feedback can accelerate your growth.

14.10 Tapping Into Other "Clairs"

Some people talk about "clairs," meaning **clairvoyance** (clear seeing), **clairaudience** (clear hearing), **clairsentience** (clear feeling), and **claircognizance** (clear knowing). You might find that you naturally gravitate towards one:

- **Clairvoyance**: Seeing mental images or visions.
- **Clairaudience**: Hearing words or sounds in your mind.
- **Clairsentience**: Feeling physical or emotional sensations.
- **Claircognizance**: Suddenly "knowing" something without knowing how.

You do not have to label these experiences as psychic if that does not fit your beliefs. You can simply notice if you get images or feelings during a Tarot reading. If it helps you interpret the cards meaningfully, it is a valuable tool.

14.11 Using Intuition When Reading for Others

14.11.1 Holding a Calm Space

When you read for someone else, your intuition can pick up on their energy, voice tone, or subtle hints in what they say. To use that effectively, try to stay calm and neutral. If you get anxious or pushy, you might project your own worries onto their reading. A calm presence allows their emotional signals to come through clearly.

14.11.2 Knowing When to Share

If your intuition tells you something sensitive—like a deep pain or a hidden fear—choose carefully how to share it. You can say, "I sense there may be some hurt you have not fully expressed," rather than blurting out a blunt statement. Respect the other person's comfort zone. Intuition is not a license to pry into private matters they are not ready to face.

14.11.3 Validating with the Cards

If you get a strong intuitive nudge that does not seem to match a card's usual meaning, see if **another card** in the spread might confirm it. For example, you sense the client is anxious about an upcoming move, even though they did not mention it. If you see the Eight of Cups in the reading, that card can indeed indicate leaving something behind or heading toward a new place. This is a sign your hunch might be on track.

14.12 Avoiding Pitfalls and Ethical Concerns

14.12.1 Making Wild Claims

While you can pick up insights, be careful about making huge claims—like diagnosing medical issues or guaranteeing big life outcomes. Tarot can guide and provide perspective, but it does not replace professional advice. If your intuition suggests someone might benefit from therapy or medical help, phrase it gently: "Have you considered talking to someone about this stress?" rather than proclaiming a strict medical conclusion.

14.12.2 Projecting Your Fears or Desires

Sometimes, you might want a certain outcome so badly that you misread the cards. For example, if you hope your friend's relationship is perfect, you might overlook cards that suggest conflict. True intuition requires honesty. If you catch yourself ignoring negative signs, step back and do a second reading or consult a neutral viewpoint. Self-awareness is key to ethical Tarot practice.

14.12.3 Respecting Boundaries

If you sense something personal about a client—like trauma or secrets—they have not shared, do not push them to reveal it. Let them decide what to disclose. Your role is to offer insights and suggestions, not to force confessions. Maintain boundaries between what you pick up intuitively and what you can respectfully discuss.

14.13 Putting It All Together

Let us walk through an example scenario to see how symbols (Chapter 13) and intuition (this chapter) work together:

1. **Question**: "How can I improve my confidence at work?"
2. **Spread**: A simple three-card layout—Situation, Advice, Outcome.
3. **Situation Card**: Three of Pentacles.
   - **Symbols**: People working together on a building, showing cooperation and skill.
   - **Intuitive Hit**: You suddenly recall a time you felt left out in a group project. This suggests your confidence issue might stem from not feeling recognized by coworkers.
4. **Advice Card**: The Queen of Wands.
   - **Symbols**: A confident woman with a sunflower, vibrant energy, possibly a cat by her side.
   - **Intuitive Hit**: You feel warmth in your chest, suggesting the card urges you to express your ideas boldly, be enthusiastic, maybe even dress in a way that makes you feel powerful.
5. **Outcome Card**: The Star.
   - **Symbols**: A woman pouring water, a large star overhead, peace.
   - **Intuitive Hit**: A sense of lightness, hope, and healing. You imagine stepping into a calmer workspace. This might confirm that if you embrace the Queen of Wands' advice, you will shine and find renewed confidence.

In this example, you used standard symbol knowledge (building for cooperation, sunflower for warmth, star for hope) and your own intuitive flashes (memory of feeling left out, a sensation of warmth). The reading becomes richer because you combined both elements.

Chapter 15: Doing a Reading for Yourself

15.1 Why Read Tarot for Yourself?

Many people start learning Tarot because they want personal guidance. They might wonder about relationships, jobs, or personal growth. Reading for yourself can be a great way to get clarity and support your own decision-making process. Unlike reading for someone else, self-readings let you explore your thoughts privately. You do not have to worry about anyone else's expectations or judgments. It can feel like having a personal journal or mirror that reflects your inner world.

At the same time, reading for yourself can be challenging. You already have strong feelings about your questions—maybe you really want a certain outcome, or perhaps you are scared of what you might see. These emotions can make it harder to stay honest and neutral while interpreting the cards. This chapter will teach you how to handle those challenges and use self-readings in a balanced way.

15.2 Getting Ready: Environment and Mindset

15.2.1 Finding a Quiet Space

When reading for yourself, it helps to find a quiet spot where you feel comfortable. This could be a small table in your room, a corner of the living room, or even a cozy seat on the floor. Make sure distractions are minimal. Turn off the TV, silence your phone if you can, and let others in your home know you need a bit of private time.

The calmer your surroundings, the easier it is to focus on the cards and your inner voice.

15.2.2 Relaxing Your Thoughts

Before shuffling, take a few slow, deep breaths. Clear your mind of rushing worries like laundry, chores, or messages on your phone. You might do a quick 30-second visualization: picture yourself setting aside all daily concerns in a little box. This mental shift can help you approach the reading with a fresh perspective. Remember, self-readings work best when you are present and open.

15.2.3 Having a Clear Question or Topic

Sometimes, you might do a reading just to see what comes up, without a specific question. That is okay. But if you have a particular issue—such as "Should I change jobs?" or "How can I handle this conflict with a friend?"—try to state that question clearly. It helps to ask open-ended questions rather than yes/no ones. For example, "What steps can I take to improve my work situation?" often yields more helpful advice than "Will I get a better job tomorrow?"

15.3 Overcoming Bias and Staying Objective

15.3.1 Recognizing Personal Bias

When reading for yourself, you might really want the cards to say something positive—like that your crush likes you back or that you will land your dream job soon. This eagerness can lead you to twist the meaning of the cards. If you see The Tower, you might pretend it is purely a good sign of "amazing changes" when it could be urging you to face a difficult upheaval first. It is normal to have hopes and fears, but you can learn to spot when they override honest interpretation.

15.3.2 Strategies to Stay Fair

- **Use a Simple Spread**: If you are very emotionally charged about a topic, try a small spread like a three-card layout. This limits how many interpretations you juggle.
- **Write Down Each Card's Meaning First**: Before you link them to your question, jot down the standard or intuitive meaning of each card as if you were reading for someone else. Then apply it to yourself.
- **Imagine You Are Reading for a Friend**: Pretend the question belongs to a friend who has the same problem. How would you interpret the cards if you were not personally involved? This can reduce emotional interference.

15.3.3 Accepting Whatever the Cards Show

Sometimes, the cards might hint at challenges or warn you about issues you do not want to face. Remember that Tarot is not "punishing" you; it is offering guidance. Accept the message, even if it is not what you hoped for. That acceptance can prevent you from cherry-picking only the happy parts. A balanced view includes both the uplifting and the cautionary.

15.4 Choosing a Spread for Self-Reading

15.4.1 Daily Draw

The **daily draw** is the simplest self-reading practice. Each morning or evening, pull one card. Ask something like, "What energy might I encounter today?" or "What do I need to reflect on tonight?" This quick habit helps you develop a personal relationship with the cards. You can note in a journal how that card's theme appeared in your day. Over time, you might see patterns—for instance, maybe The Hermit shows up whenever you feel stressed and need alone time.

15.4.2 Three-Card Check-In

A **three-card check-in** can give more detail than a single draw. You could designate the positions as:

1. **Current State**: Where am I emotionally or mentally right now?
2. **Challenge**: What is blocking me or complicating my situation?
3. **Advice**: How can I move forward?

Alternatively, you can set them as **Past, Present, Future** if you want a timeline perspective. The key is to keep it simple. Fewer cards often mean fewer chances for confusion or bias when you are reading for yourself.

15.4.3 Larger Spreads with Caution

There is nothing wrong with using a bigger spread like the Celtic Cross for a self-reading, especially if you have a complex issue. However, it is easier to get overwhelmed by details or let your wishes color your interpretations. If you do choose a big spread, go slowly. Interpret each position carefully, and maybe take breaks if you feel stuck or anxious. Writing down your thoughts can help you maintain clarity.

15.5 Interpreting the Cards: Practical Tips

15.5.1 Journaling for Self-Reflection

When reading for yourself, journaling can be a game changer. For each card you draw, note:

- **What you see**: Describe the image and symbols plainly.
- **What you feel**: Note any emotions or bodily reactions.
- **Possible meaning**: Combine the card's basic definition with your intuition.
- **How it applies**: Relate it to your question or your life right now.

Journaling slows you down so you do not jump to "Oh, this is clearly good news!" or "That means I am doomed." Instead, you explore methodically. Over time, you build a record of your personal growth and how your self-readings align with real-life events.

15.5.2 Clarifier Cards

If a certain card confuses you, you can pull a **clarifier card**. For instance, if you get The Moon in the advice position and are unsure whether it is urging you to trust your intuition or warning you about illusions, you might draw one extra card to clarify. This second card can add context. However, do not go overboard pulling clarifiers for every single card. You can quickly spiral into more confusion or keep fishing for a "better" outcome.

15.5.3 Combining Intellect with Emotion

Use both your **logical mind** (knowing typical card meanings) and your **emotional or intuitive mind** (seeing how the card feels to you). For instance, the Four of Cups might traditionally mean boredom or missing opportunities. Intuitively, you might feel a sense of quiet reflection. Maybe in this reading, it is more about pausing to see blessings you have been ignoring. Balancing these two views creates a fuller interpretation that suits your personal situation.

15.6 Handling Difficult Topics

15.6.1 Facing Hard Truths

Self-readings can bring up sensitive issues—like heartbreak, past traumas, or fears about the future. If you draw cards that point to painful truths, give yourself permission to pause, reflect, or come back later. Tarot is a tool for insight, not self-punishment. You do not have to solve everything at once. Sometimes, just acknowledging a problem is the first step toward healing.

15.6.2 Knowing Your Limits

If a topic is too intense—such as severe mental health issues or major life crises—remember that Tarot is not a substitute for professional help. You can still do a reading to explore your emotions, but also consider talking to a counselor, therapist, or trusted mentor. Self-readings can guide you, but they are not meant to replace medical, legal, or psychological advice.

15.6.3 Self-Compassion

Always read for yourself with **kindness**. If you see a card combination that suggests setbacks or emotional pain, practice self-compassion. Speak to yourself as you would to a dear friend: "I see this is a tough situation. Let's figure out how to support ourselves through this." That supportive mindset makes the reading more healing rather than discouraging.

15.7 Developing a Self-Reading Routine

15.7.1 Frequency of Readings

How often should you read for yourself? It varies. Some people draw one card every day. Others do a longer spread once a week. If you find daily draws are too much or lead to overthinking, scale back. There is no hard rule. A moderate approach can help you avoid obsessing over every small event with repeated readings.

15.7.2 Setting Goals or Intentions

You can use self-readings to track goals. For example, if you are working on improving your fitness, you might ask, "What energy should I embrace this week to stay motivated?" Or if you are learning a new skill, "What can help me overcome my fears about trying something unfamiliar?" By focusing your reading on constructive questions, you align Tarot with personal growth rather than using it purely for predicting outcomes.

15.7.3 Reviewing Past Readings

From time to time, look back at your Tarot journal. See if earlier readings connect with events that happened. Notice if your interpretation style has changed. Celebrate improvements—like how you handled a problem after seeing The Chariot, or how you recognized a Tower moment and came out stronger. Reflecting on past readings can build confidence in your ability to interpret the cards honestly.

15.8 Example Self-Reading Walkthrough

Imagine you are feeling stuck in your career. You decide to do a **three-card spread** asking, "What do I need to know about moving forward in my career?"

1. **Shuffle** and focus on your question: "How can I move forward in my career?"
2. **Layout**: Three cards representing (1) Current Challenge, (2) Guidance, (3) Possible Outcome.

- **Card 1: Eight of Swords**
    - Traditional Meaning: Feeling trapped or limited by your own mindset.
    - Self-Reflection: "I might be overthinking my options or doubting my abilities."
    - Journal Note: "I feel anxious when I see this card, which fits the trapped figure. Maybe I am my own biggest obstacle."
- **Card 2: Knight of Wands**
    - Traditional Meaning: Bold action, courage, passion for new projects.
    - Self-Reflection: "This card makes me feel an excited energy. It suggests I need to be more daring. Perhaps apply for positions I find interesting even if they are a stretch."
    - Journal Note: "I sense I should break routine, maybe attend a networking event or try a new approach at work."
- **Card 3: The Empress**
    - Traditional Meaning: Creativity, growth, nurturing success.
    - Self-Reflection: "I see abundance and potential. This could indicate a satisfying career path if I trust my creativity."

- - Journal Note: "I feel comfort. Maybe I can find a role that supports my need for a balanced, nurturing environment."

Overall Interpretation: "Right now, I am limiting myself (Eight of Swords). The guidance is to be bold like the Knight of Wands, maybe shake off fear and try something new. The outcome, The Empress, suggests growth and creativity if I follow that guidance."

This self-reading gave you insights about your mindset, the action you can take, and a sense of a positive future if you move forward confidently.

15.9 When Self-Readings Become Confusing

15.9.1 Stepping Away

Sometimes, you might do a reading and feel more confused than before. That is okay. Take a break. Go for a walk, do something fun, or switch tasks. Come back later and see if your interpretation changes. Clarity can emerge once you are not overthinking.

15.9.2 Asking a Friend or Tarot Community

If you feel really stuck, you can share your reading (minus personal details if you prefer privacy) with a trusted friend who also studies Tarot. Ask for their perspective. Sometimes, an outside viewpoint can break through self-bias. There are also online Tarot communities where people give feedback on spreads. Just remember that ultimately, your own insight should guide you. Others can offer suggestions, but you know your life best.

15.9.3 Avoid Repeatedly Asking the Same Question

If you keep drawing cards for the same question day after day, you might get jumbled answers, or the cards might repeat themselves. It is like pestering a friend with the same question—they might give you the same advice or grow silent. If you do not like an answer, it might be tempting to keep asking until you get a favorable card. That usually leads to confusion. Trust the answer you got, or wait until circumstances genuinely change before asking again.

Chapter 16: Doing a Reading for Others

16.1 What Makes Reading for Others Different?

Reading Tarot for someone else can feel like an exciting step in your journey. You shift from personal self-reflection to helping another person explore their concerns. This requires new skills: **clear communication**, **listening**, and **respect** for the other person's boundaries. You are no longer the only one affected by the reading. Your interpretations might shape their decisions or bring up hidden emotions. That means you carry a bit more responsibility.

In many ways, reading for others can also help you grow as a Tarot reader. You see how the cards speak to different life stories. You might discover new angles on familiar cards. And you learn about empathy—how to sense what your friend or client is going through without imposing your own opinions. This chapter will walk you through practical steps for reading Tarot with other people in mind, whether they are close friends or complete strangers seeking guidance.

16.2 Preparing Yourself and the Other Person

16.2.1 Checking Your Readiness

Before you offer to read for others, ask yourself: **Am I comfortable with the basics of Tarot?** You do not need to be an expert, but you should have enough familiarity with card meanings and basic spreads so you do not freeze up during the reading. It is also helpful if you have done enough self-readings to feel confident in your interpretive process. Reading for others can be a learning experience, but you want some foundation.

16.2.2 Setting Up the Space

If you are reading in person:

- **Choose a calm area**: A kitchen table, a quiet corner at a café, a small office—somewhere you can lay out cards without too much disruption.
- **Minimize distractions**: Turn off loud music, silence your phone, and ask if they mind you lighting a candle or playing soft background music (if that helps both of you relax).
- **Comfortable seating**: Sit across from each other or side by side. Make sure you both can see the cards.

If reading online (via video call), try to ensure good lighting so they can see the cards when you hold them up. Check audio quality. Explain how you will shuffle, lay out the cards, and share your interpretations on camera.

16.2.3 Clarifying Expectations

Talk briefly with the other person about **what they want** from the reading. Are they seeking general insight, or do they have a specific question? Do they expect a quick 5-minute overview or a deeper 30-minute session? Make sure you both agree on the focus and length. If someone says they want to know "everything about the future," gently guide them to a more workable question, like "What do I need to know about this coming year?" Setting realistic expectations helps avoid misunderstandings later.

16.3 Gathering the Question or Topic

16.3.1 Encouraging Open-Ended Questions

For many readings, open-ended questions like, "What can help me resolve conflicts in my relationship?" or "How can I find more fulfillment in my job?" yield richer insights than yes/no questions. If the person initially asks, "Will I get married this year?" you might reframe it as, "What do I need to know about finding or nurturing a healthy relationship?" This shift moves the reading from pure prediction to deeper guidance.

16.3.2 Respecting Privacy

Sometimes, a person might not want to share all the details. That is okay. You can do a general reading with minimal information. If you sense they are holding back something important, you can politely ask if they feel comfortable clarifying. But never push or pry. It is their choice to reveal as much or as little as they wish. Tarot readings can still be meaningful with limited details.

16.3.3 Handling Sensitive Topics

If the question is about serious issues—like legal matters, major health concerns, or life-and-death situations—remember that Tarot is not a replacement for professional advice. You can offer emotional support or perspective on how they feel about the situation, but do not pretend to be a doctor, lawyer, or financial expert. Gently remind them to seek qualified help if needed.

16.4 Shuffling and Involving the Querent

16.4.1 Letting Them Shuffle (If In Person)

Some readers like to have the other person (often called the **querent**) shuffle the cards. This can help them feel more connected to the reading. If they seem unsure how to shuffle, teach them a simple overhand method or suggest they mix the cards on the table. Alternatively, if you prefer to keep your deck to yourself, you can shuffle while having them focus on their question. Either way is fine—choose what feels comfortable and respectful.

16.4.2 Intentional Cutting

If you do not want them to shuffle, you can still let them **cut the deck** after you shuffle. They pick how to split the deck (into two or three piles), then you restack them. This small action allows them to influence the final order of the cards. Some believe it ties their energy to the reading. Whether or not you see it as literal "energy," it can psychologically involve them, which is often a positive step.

16.4.3 Explaining as You Go

If the person is new to Tarot, they might be curious about why you are shuffling a certain way or how many times you do it. Feel free to give a brief explanation: "I like to shuffle until I sense it is mixed well," or "I am thinking about your question while I shuffle." This transparency builds trust and demystifies the process.

16.5 Choosing and Explaining the Spread

16.5.1 Match the Spread to the Question

If they have a quick question, a **three-card spread** might be enough. For deeper exploration, you could use something like the **Celtic Cross** or a specialized layout for relationships or career. Briefly describe the spread: "We will draw 10 cards in the Celtic Cross. The first two show your main situation and obstacles, the next few explore deeper factors, and the final card looks at the potential outcome." Clarity helps the querent follow along.

16.5.2 Laying Out Cards One by One

When you place the cards, do so calmly. Some readers like to flip each card as they lay it down, while others place them all face-down first and then flip them in order. Explain the meaning of each position as you go: "This card shows your past influences," "This one is the advice the Tarot offers." That way, the querent understands why each card matters.

16.5.3 Encourage Interaction

You can invite the querent to share their thoughts: "Does this card remind you of anything in your life?" or "How does this image make you feel?" This conversation can spark personal connections. Sometimes they might say, "That looks just like my office situation!" or "I feel uneasy about those swords." These reactions are gold. They reveal how the querent's own experiences link to the Tarot symbols.

16.6 Interpreting with Care and Compassion

16.6.1 Describing the Cards in Simple Terms

Try not to overwhelm the querent with obscure jargon. Instead of saying, "This indicates a Saturnian influence in your 8th house, meaning karmic transformations," you could say, "This card suggests big changes that might feel tough at first but can lead to a better understanding of your deeper fears and strengths." Use language that is easy to understand. You can always mention the "fancy" terms if you like, but be sure to clarify them.

16.6.2 Balancing Positive and Challenging Insights

If the reading shows difficult themes—like heartbreak, conflict, or big transitions—share them gently but honestly. Give the querent space to react. You might say, "This card can indicate a struggle or some sadness. Does that resonate with anything happening in your life?" Let them respond. Then, look for constructive advice or hopeful angles in the other cards. It is rarely just bad news. Even The Tower can mean a needed breakthrough or the end of shaky foundations.

16.6.3 Avoiding Absolute Statements

Phrases like "You will definitely lose your job" or "This person is 100% the one you will marry" can be risky. Life is full of free will and changing circumstances. A more balanced approach might be, "These cards show potential conflicts at work, so be cautious. Focus on communication and problem-solving if you want to avoid bigger issues." By framing it this way, you empower the querent to take action rather than feeling helpless.

16.7 Handling Emotions and Questions

16.7.1 Listening Actively

Reading for others involves good listening skills. If the querent becomes emotional—maybe they tear up or get frustrated—pause and let them process. Ask gently, "Do you want a moment, or do you have any thoughts about what we have seen so far?" This shows you care about their feelings. Active listening creates a safe environment for them to share or reflect.

16.7.2 Dealing with Skepticism or Nervousness

Some people might be anxious or skeptical about Tarot. They might say, "I am not sure I believe in this," or "I am scared to hear something bad." Reassure them that Tarot is not about doom or guaranteeing events. It is a tool for guidance and self-reflection. Encourage them to see it as a conversation starter about their life. If they remain uncomfortable, you can politely shorten the reading or invite them to end it if they wish.

16.7.3 Answering Follow-Up Questions

Once the spread is interpreted, the querent might ask, "What if I do not want that outcome?" or "Can the cards tell me more about my love life specifically?" You can draw **clarifier cards** or do a smaller follow-up spread. Just be sure not to drag on indefinitely. If they keep asking the same question in different forms, suggest they take time to digest what they already got. Repeated queries might lead to confusion.

16.8 Ethics and Boundaries

16.8.1 Privacy and Confidentiality

If someone shares personal issues during a reading, respect that information. Do not gossip about it to mutual friends or post it online without permission. Treat their story with care and keep it private. This builds trust and shows you take their well-being seriously.

16.8.2 Declining Certain Topics

You might decide not to read on certain topics—such as serious health diagnoses, legal judgments, or third-party privacy issues (like "Is my coworker cheating on their partner?"). It is okay to set boundaries: "I am sorry, but I do not do readings about other people's private lives without their permission," or "I am not qualified to give medical or legal advice." You can gently redirect them to a professional or suggest focusing on how they can cope emotionally.

16.8.3 Handling Predictive Questions Carefully

Predicting exact future events can be tricky. Some readers prefer focusing on guidance and possible outcomes rather than definitive statements. If someone insists, "Tell me exactly when I will meet my soulmate," you can say, "Tarot can describe energies and potentials, but you also have free will. Let us see what the cards advise about finding meaningful connections." This approach encourages them to stay active in shaping their life.

16.9 Reading for Strangers vs. Friends

16.9.1 Reading for Friends

Pros: You already know their context, which can make it easier to interpret.
Cons: Personal bias might creep in—maybe you want them to break up with their partner, so you read the cards that way.

To handle this, try to keep an open mind. If a friend's reading suggests something that goes against your personal opinion, present it calmly. "Even though I personally feel concerned about your relationship, these cards suggest there might be a chance for healing if both parties are willing."

16.9.2 Reading for Strangers

Pros: Less bias, a fresh view of their situation.
Cons: They might need more explanation of your process, and building trust can take effort.

Ask polite, open-ended questions about what they want to explore. Offer short clarifications about how you read cards. Focus on creating a welcoming atmosphere where they feel safe to share. If they are extremely private, just use the cards to describe possible energies and let them decide how it fits their life.

16.10 Conducting an Online or Phone Reading

16.10.1 Technology Setup

If reading through video chat, confirm the internet connection and audio are stable. A phone or webcam that clearly shows the cards helps the querent feel engaged. If reading by phone only (no video), describe each card: "I have drawn The Star—it shows a woman pouring water, a large star overhead. It often means hope and guidance." Be detailed so they can visualize.

16.10.2 Maintaining Connection

Try to keep the conversation natural. Ask if they have questions after you interpret each card or group of cards. Without face-to-face cues, it might be harder to sense their reactions, so encourage them to speak up if something does not make sense. Pause regularly to check in: "Does this resonate with you? Do you see how it might apply to your situation?"

16.10.3 Respecting Time and Boundaries

Online readings can easily run long if you are both at home and comfortable. Still, set a reasonable time limit, like 30 minutes or an hour. End the session politely when time is up. If the querent wants another reading or deeper exploration, schedule a future session. Maintaining boundaries ensures you do not burn out or push them into information overload.

16.11 Troubleshooting Common Challenges

16.11.1 Querent Disagrees with the Reading

Sometimes, a querent says, "That does not ring true at all." Avoid getting defensive. You might politely ask if any part of the reading resonates or if they are willing to see if it unfolds later. If they remain certain it is off-track, you can accept that. Tarot is interpretive, and not every reading hits the mark perfectly. Encourage them to reflect on it over time or discuss any angles you might have missed.

16.11.2 Querent Becomes Overly Dependent

If a person comes to you repeatedly for every small decision, you can gently remind them that Tarot is a tool, not a substitute for their own judgment or professional help. Suggest they take some space to apply the advice from the current reading. If they still press for constant readings, consider setting limits—like only once a month or once a week. This prevents an unhealthy dependence.

16.11.3 Feeling Drained or Overwhelmed

Reading for others can be draining, especially if the topic is heavy or you do multiple readings in a row. Take breaks, drink water, and ground yourself after each session. Some people do a quick "shake out" of their hands or short breathing exercise to release the emotional energy. Self-care ensures you can continue offering quality readings without burning out.

16.12 Example: A Simple Friend Reading

Imagine your friend, Anna, asks about her new job. She is excited but worried about fitting in with the team. You decide on a **three-card spread** for clarity.

1. **Anna Shuffles** while thinking, "How can I best adjust to my new workplace?"
2. She cuts the deck, you restack.
3. **Card 1 (The Challenge)**: Five of Wands—symbolizing competition or minor conflicts.
   - You explain: "This might show that the team environment has different personalities. There could be friendly rivalry or group debates that feel stressful."
   - Anna nods, saying it is a competitive company.
4. **Card 2 (Advice)**: Page of Pentacles—youthful, focused approach.
   - You say: "This suggests approaching tasks with a learning mindset. Be eager, ask questions, show you are willing to grow. That can win respect in a busy team."
   - Anna says she was afraid to appear inexperienced, but maybe asking for help is okay.
5. **Card 3 (Likely Outcome)**: Three of Cups—celebration, camaraderie.
   - You interpret: "If you follow the Page's advice, you might find supportive friendships and a sense of teamwork. The Three of Cups often indicates social harmony and shared success."
   - Anna smiles, relieved that it points to a positive connection with coworkers.

You end the reading by summarizing: "Starting might be stressful (Five of Wands), but if you stay open and curious (Page of Pentacles), you can build friendships and enjoy your new workplace (Three of Cups)."

16.13 Wrapping Up the Reading and Follow-Through

16.13.1 Summarizing Key Points

After going through the spread, offer a concise summary: "So, we see that you are facing a bit of competition, but you have the potential to learn and blend well with the team if you remain open-minded." This helps the querent remember the main message.

16.13.2 Asking If They Have Final Questions

Give them a moment to ask anything else or clarify any part of the reading they did not understand. Sometimes they might say, "Wait, can we revisit Card 2? I want to be sure how it fits my situation." A final check-in ensures they leave the session feeling informed.

16.13.3 Positive Encouragement

Even if challenging cards appear, end on a supportive note. You might say, "I see you have the strength to handle this. The cards suggest you have the resources to make wise choices." Encouragement does not mean sugarcoating. It means acknowledging their power to shape their path going forward.

Chapter 17: Ethics and Responsibility in Tarot

17.1 Why Ethics Matter in Tarot

Tarot is more than just a deck of cards; it is a practice that can touch people's hearts and minds. When you do a Tarot reading—whether for yourself or for others—you are dealing with sensitive topics like feelings, fears, and dreams. This is why **ethics** (right and fair behavior) and **responsibility** (being careful with the power you hold) are so important. You do not have to be an expert or a psychic to realize that your words can deeply affect another person.

- **Ethics**: How we treat others with respect and honesty.
- **Responsibility**: Recognizing the impact of our words and actions, and using them thoughtfully.

Sometimes, people use Tarot for fun. But even a "fun" reading can stir up emotions or raise concerns. If you tell someone the cards show trouble, they might worry a lot. If you promise them a glorious future, they might cling to false hope. That does not mean you can never talk about hard truths or positive possibilities—it just means you should do it in a way that is respectful, caring, and honest.

17.2 Respecting Boundaries and Privacy

17.2.1 Personal Information

When someone comes to you for a reading, they might share personal details: a difficult breakup, a job worry, or a family conflict.

Keep that information private. It is not your story to tell others. If a friend asks, "What did they say about their breakup?" you can politely respond, "I am sorry, that is confidential." Respecting someone's story builds trust and shows you value their privacy.

17.2.2 Emotional Sensitivity

Tarot readings can bring up strong feelings. You might see tears, anger, or relief. As a responsible reader, you give the other person space to feel and process. Do not rush them or force them to open up more than they want to. Some people may only want a quick insight; others want a heart-to-heart talk. Notice their comfort level. If they start looking anxious or uneasy, you can pause: "Are you okay to continue?" This shows you care about their emotional well-being.

17.2.3 Reading About Third Parties

It is tempting to ask, "Is my ex happy with their new partner?" or "Is my coworker planning to quit?" But reading about someone who has not given permission can feel invasive. It is like peeking into their private life without their consent. A more respectful approach is to focus on your own relationship with that person. For instance: "How can I heal from this breakup?" or "How can I improve my work situation?" That way, you stay within ethical lines by centering on what you can control—your own actions and feelings.

17.3 Consent: Asking Before Reading

17.3.1 Getting Permission

Consent means making sure the person actually wants a reading. Maybe you have a friend who is skeptical or who has had bad experiences with "fortune telling." Do not push a reading on them. Ask politely: "I have my Tarot cards with me—would you like some insight?" If they say no, respect that answer. Forcing a Tarot reading can cause discomfort or distrust.

17.3.2 Children and Younger People

If a child or young teenager is curious about Tarot, be extra cautious. Make sure you have permission from a parent or guardian before doing a reading for them. Also, keep the reading simple and gentle. Avoid scary language or heavy topics. Children's imaginations are powerful, and you do not want them to worry about "curses" or scary predictions. Focus on uplifting messages, such as building confidence or understanding feelings.

17.3.3 Public Demonstrations

Sometimes, you might do readings at a party or community event. Let people come to you rather than cornering them with, "Sit down—I'll read your future!" Have a small sign that says "Tarot Readings" and greet anyone who approaches with a friendly explanation: "I'm here if you want some guidance or insight." Giving them the choice to opt in or out respects their autonomy.

17.4 Honesty and Clarity

17.4.1 Avoiding Exaggerated Claims

It is fun to talk about mystical powers or psychic visions, but be honest about what you can actually offer. If you are not a medium who talks to spirits, do not pretend you are. If someone asks, "Are you 100% sure this will happen?" you can say, "Tarot shows possibilities and guidance. We also have free will to change outcomes." Honesty prevents misunderstandings and keeps the reading grounded.

17.4.2 Disclaimers for Legal and Medical Issues

If a person asks about legal, medical, or financial problems, remind them: "I am not a doctor/lawyer/financial advisor. Tarot can explore how you might feel about your choices, but it is not a substitute for professional advice." This little disclaimer can protect both you and them. You are not claiming to be an authority on serious matters outside your skill set. You are simply offering emotional or spiritual insights.

17.4.3 Handling Predictions Carefully

Cards like The Tower, Death, or Three of Swords can look scary. While they can hint at challenges, do not present them as doom. For example, you could say, "This card can mean a sudden change or something ending, but it often leads to a fresh start or positive shift once the dust settles." By balancing honesty (yes, it might be tough) with optimism (there can be growth), you respect the querent's feelings while staying true to the card's symbolic range.

17.5 Being Mindful with Vulnerable People

17.5.1 Emotional Vulnerability

Some folks approach Tarot when they are at a low point—after a breakup, job loss, or during emotional stress. You hold a big responsibility in how you guide them. Do not exploit their fears by making them buy extra services or scaring them with curses. That is unethical. Instead, offer supportive insights and, if needed, gently suggest seeking professional help like counseling for deeper issues.

17.5.2 Cultural Sensitivities

Tarot has roots in various cultures and has been shaped by many traditions. If you work with someone from a culture that views Tarot differently—maybe they see it as taboo or extremely sacred—be respectful. Learn about their beliefs, listen to their concerns, and do not dismiss them. Show that you value their viewpoint. If they decide not to pursue a Tarot reading based on their cultural beliefs, respect that choice.

17.5.3 People with Mental Health Challenges

Tarot can be a tool for self-reflection, but it is not a mental health treatment. If you sense someone is struggling with severe anxiety, depression, or other mental health issues, approach the reading gently. Do not try to diagnose them. Encourage them to speak with a licensed therapist or psychologist if their struggles are intense. Offer compassion, but know your limits.

17.6 Charging for Readings or Offering for Free

17.6.1 Value Exchange

Some readers do Tarot as a hobby, reading for friends without charging. Others make it a professional service. If you choose to charge, think about how you set your price. Consider your experience level, time spent, and local market rates if applicable. The key is to be transparent: let people know upfront if there is a cost. If you prefer donations or bartering (like exchanging a reading for a homemade meal), that is also fine—just be clear about expectations.

17.6.2 Fairness and Refunds

What if someone pays for a reading and feels unsatisfied? One approach is to offer a partial refund, a shorter follow-up reading, or a polite explanation that Tarot is interpretive and not always exact. If you keep your conditions honest—like "I will do my best to interpret the cards, but I cannot guarantee specific results"—people often appreciate the sincerity. Having a simple refund or no-refund policy stated in advance avoids confusion.

17.6.3 No Pressure Tactics

It is unethical to pressure someone into buying more readings with scare tactics like, "I sense a curse, and only another $50 reading can remove it." This manipulative behavior has given Tarot a bad name in some circles. Be aware that your role is to give insight and guidance, not to frighten people into spending money. If you see a potential issue, discuss it kindly, focusing on solutions and the querent's free will rather than doom.

17.7 Taking Care of Yourself as a Reader

17.7.1 Avoiding Burnout

Reading for others, especially about heavy topics, can be draining. You might absorb their emotions or worries. To stay ethical, you need to keep your own mental health in check. Schedule breaks, limit how many readings you do in one day, and find ways to recharge—like meditation, hobbies, or chatting with supportive friends. You cannot help others well if you are exhausted or emotionally overwhelmed.

17.7.2 Personal Boundaries

If a client or friend messages you at midnight asking for an urgent reading, you do not have to say yes. Setting boundaries like business hours (even if you are not a full-time professional) is okay. You can say, "I am available on weekends or between 6–8 pm." Being constantly on call can lead to stress or resentment. An ethical reader respects both the querent's needs and their own well-being.

17.7.3 Continuous Learning

Ethical responsibility also means staying open to growth. You can read books, watch instructional videos, or talk to experienced Tarot readers about ethical dilemmas. Learn from your mistakes. If you ever realize you said something hurtful or misleading, own up to it and do better next time. Being ethical is a journey, not a one-time achievement.

17.8 Cultural Respect and Avoiding Appropriation

17.8.1 Understanding Tarot's Global Influences

Tarot has been shaped by European history, occult traditions, and modern interpretations from around the world. If you incorporate elements from different cultures—like smudging with sage (related to some Indigenous practices) or referencing Eastern religious concepts—do so respectfully. Acknowledge the sources, learn the context, and avoid trivializing sacred rituals. This thoughtfulness shows you value the roots of your practice.

17.8.2 Avoiding Offensive Decks or Imagery

Some decks may contain stereotypes or harmful portrayals of cultural or religious groups. If you use such a deck, reflect on whether it offends or misrepresents people. You might choose to retire that deck, modify it, or discuss the issue openly. Ethics means being mindful that images have power, and misusing them can perpetuate prejudice or disrespect.

17.9 Balancing Support and Free Will

17.9.1 Empowering the Querent

An ethical reader does not dictate decisions. Instead of "You must break up with your partner," say, "These cards suggest ongoing conflict—here are some ways you might handle it. Ultimately, you know your situation best." This language respects the querent's free will. It reminds them that Tarot is not an absolute judge but a guide to possible paths.

17.9.2 Offering Possible Paths

When the cards show challenges, it can help to present various outcomes. For instance, "If you remain in your current job without addressing issues, the stress might continue. If you choose to communicate your concerns or look for a different role, you might find relief. This is what the cards seem to indicate." Laying out multiple approaches fosters healthy decision-making rather than telling them there is only one correct way.

17.9.3 Recognizing When to Refer

Sometimes, the cards highlight serious issues—like signs of addiction, abusive relationships, or deep trauma. You might see a pattern suggesting the querent needs professional counseling or community support. You can gently say, "Tarot is showing me there is significant pain here that may need more help than a card reading can provide. I encourage you to consider talking with a counselor or a trusted professional." Suggesting resources is caring and ethical.

17.10 Summary of Ethical Principles

1. **Confidentiality**: Keep personal stories private.
2. **Consent**: Only read for those who agree.
3. **Honesty**: Be clear about what you can and cannot do; avoid pretending to be something you are not.
4. **Boundaries**: Set limits on your availability, the topics you are comfortable covering, and how you handle emotional or cultural issues.
5. **No Exploitation**: Do not use fear or manipulation to make money or gain control over someone.
6. **Respect for Cultures**: Be mindful of the origins of practices and any potential stereotyping in your deck or reading style.
7. **Empowerment**: Present information so the querent can decide what is best for them, rather than commanding them.
8. **Self-Care**: Maintain your own well-being to remain compassionate and fair.

When you follow these principles, you create a safe environment for yourself and for anyone who seeks your readings. You show that Tarot can be a respectful, uplifting experience rather than a source of fear or confusion.

Chapter 18: Overcoming Reading Challenges

18.1 Why Reading Challenges Happen

Every Tarot reader—beginner or expert—runs into moments where they feel stuck or confused. You might draw a spread that seems contradictory or get a question that is so broad, you do not know where to start. Challenges can also appear when the querent is skeptical, emotional, or not providing enough information. Rather than seeing these as failures, look at them as opportunities to refine your skills. When you learn how to handle tricky situations, you become more creative, patient, and flexible.

Common Reasons for Reading Challenges:

- The question is unclear or too broad.
- Emotions (yours or the querent's) are running high.
- The cards seem to contradict each other.
- The querent expects exact predictions.
- Personal bias clouds your judgment.
- The reading environment is distracting.

In this chapter, we will explore common roadblocks and offer practical strategies to overcome them. By staying calm, using the tools we have discussed, and trusting the process, you can guide even the toughest reading to a helpful conclusion.

18.2 Confusing or Contradictory Cards

18.2.1 Example of Contradiction

You pull a spread about someone's career path. One card suggests speed and bold action (like the Knight of Wands), while the next card suggests caution and patience (like the Four of Swords). It looks like they are telling two opposite stories: "Hurry up!" vs. "Slow down!"

18.2.2 Possible Explanations

1. **Different aspects of the same situation**: Maybe the querent should act boldly in seeking new opportunities (Knight of Wands), but also make sure to rest and not burn out (Four of Swords).
2. **Internal vs. External**: One card might reflect the querent's internal drive, the other might reflect external factors. The spread can be showing a tug-of-war between wanting to move quickly and the reality that a careful approach is needed.
3. **Timing**: The Knight of Wands might apply to the immediate step (pitching an idea now), while the Four of Swords might suggest a recovery period afterward.

18.2.3 How to Resolve

- **Look at the Spread Positions**: Are they assigned roles (e.g., "Advice" vs. "Obstacle")? That can clarify each card's function.
- **Pull a Clarifier Card**: If truly stuck, draw one extra card to see how these energies interact.
- **Blend the Messages**: Instead of deciding which card is "right," think about how both energies could coexist. Often, the message is multi-layered.

18.3 Emotional Overload in a Reading

18.3.1 Recognizing Emotional Tension

You might notice the querent is on the verge of tears or is extremely anxious. Maybe they ask about a painful breakup or a recent loss. If they start crying or shaking, it is okay to pause. Hand them tissues, offer a moment of quiet. Reading Tarot is not a race. Let them breathe and gather themselves.

18.3.2 Handling the Moment

- **Validate**: Gently say, "I see this is tough for you. It is alright to feel sad or overwhelmed."
- **Pause the Reading**: Ask if they want to take a break or continue. Some people need a few minutes to calm down.
- **Simplify the Spread**: If you planned a big 10-card layout, maybe switch to a simpler 3-card approach. Overloading them with complex interpretations can add stress.
- **Offer Comfort, Not Therapy**: You can be kind, but you are not a trained therapist (unless you are!). Suggest professional help if it seems needed.

18.3.3 Protecting Your Own Emotions

If you also get emotional—maybe their situation hits close to home—take a mental step back. Ground yourself by focusing on your breathing, reminding yourself you are there to guide, not to drown in their feelings. After the reading, do something calming: go for a walk, journal, or do a quick meditation.

18.4 Querent Disengagement or Skepticism

18.4.1 Signs of Disengagement

The querent might fold their arms, answer with curt replies, or repeatedly say, "I don't believe in this stuff." They may have been dragged there by a friend or are just curious but not open. Skepticism can be healthy, but it can also block them from truly exploring what the cards might offer.

18.4.2 Approaches

- **Respect Their View**: Acknowledge it: "It is okay to be skeptical. Tarot can be seen as a tool for reflection rather than absolute predictions. We can still see if anything resonates."
- **Ask Questions**: Invite them to pick a topic important to them. Even a skeptic might open up if they have a real concern in mind.
- **Keep It Simple**: Do a quick 3-card reading. Overloading them with esoteric details might increase their doubt. Focus on practical insights, like how to handle a problem at work or find balance in life.
- **No Need to Prove**: You are not obligated to convert them into a believer. If they remain closed off, that is their choice. Offer the reading calmly, and if they dismiss it, accept that outcome.

18.5 Overly Vague or Giant Questions

18.5.1 Examples of Vague Questions

- "Tell me everything about my life."
- "What is going to happen in the next 20 years?"
- "I want to know my entire future."

Such questions are too broad. The Tarot works best with a focus—like a specific area (relationships, career, personal growth) or a timeframe (the next few months). Trying to cover every detail of someone's whole life in one reading is overwhelming.

18.5.2 How to Narrow It Down

- **Help Them Reframe**: "What part of your life feels most important right now?" or "Which area do you want the most clarity on?"
- **Use a General Spread**: If they insist on a general reading, use a spread that touches multiple life areas, like a 5-card or 7-card layout with positions for relationships, career, health, etc. Then you can mention each area briefly.
- **Suggest Multiple Readings**: Sometimes, they want a big overview. You could do a broad reading, then recommend separate, smaller readings for specific topics.

18.6 Dealing with Negative or "Scary" Cards

18.6.1 Examples of "Scary" Cards

- **Death**: Often about transformation or endings.
- **The Tower**: Sudden upheaval, possible crisis leading to breakthroughs.

- **Ten of Swords**: A painful ending or betrayal.
- **Three of Swords**: Heartache or sadness.

Querents might gasp or panic upon seeing these. They might fear literal death or ruin.

18.6.2 Reassuring Interpretation

Remind them that these cards can be calls to action or signals of needed change. **Death** can be the end of a bad habit, not a literal passing. **The Tower** can be a wake-up call to break free from a shaky foundation. Focus on growth potential. Let them know these cards are part of life's ups and downs, and they often lead to a better place after the storm.

18.6.3 Suggesting Steps

If the reading suggests a tough phase, encourage practical steps. For instance: "If The Tower appears for your job situation, maybe it is time to have an honest conversation with your boss or consider new opportunities. This card can mean a shake-up is on the horizon, but you have the power to adapt."

18.7 When Personal Bias Interferes

18.7.1 Recognizing Your Bias

Maybe you strongly dislike your friend's partner, so you automatically interpret the cards as signs they should break up. Or you hate your own job, so you assume that any job question must end with "Leave the job!" Step back and ask if the cards themselves truly support that conclusion or if you are forcing it.

18.7.2 How to Stay Neutral

- **Focus on the Symbols**: Stick to what you see in the card imagery. If you start going off-track, ask yourself if it is the card speaking or your personal opinion.
- **Imagine Someone Else**: Pretend a stranger asked the same question. Would you interpret the cards the same way?
- **Seek a Second Opinion**: If you are truly stuck, you could show the spread to another reader (with the querent's permission or while keeping them anonymous). Ask how they would interpret it.

18.7.3 Apologizing If Necessary

If you realize after the reading that you let your bias overshadow the messages, consider a polite follow-up: "I was thinking about your reading, and I realize I might have pushed my personal feelings in. I want to clarify that the cards could also indicate…" Owning up to mistakes can deepen trust rather than harm it.

18.8 Repeated or "Stuck" Questions

18.8.1 Querent Keeps Asking the Same Thing

Sometimes, a querent is fixated on one issue—like "Will my ex come back?"—and they ask repeatedly. They might keep hoping the cards will show a different result. This can lead to circular readings that all say the same thing, or become more confusing over time.

18.8.2 Setting Limits

You can gently say, "We have explored that question in depth. Let us give it some time before we ask again, or look at a different angle." If they persist, you might refuse another reading on the exact same topic until a certain time has passed. This boundary helps avoid draining your energy and feeding their anxiety.

18.8.3 Helping Them Reflect

Suggest journaling or taking real-life steps. For instance: "The cards often mention communication issues. Maybe try writing a letter to your ex or focusing on self-care. Then check in a couple of weeks to see if anything has changed." Encouraging action is better than re-reading the same spread daily.

18.9 Handling "No Connection" Situations

18.9.1 Feeling Zero Resonance

Once in a while, you or the querent might feel nothing fits. The reading just does not click. The cards do not seem relevant, or the querent is stone-faced. This can happen for several reasons: the querent is not ready to open up, the question is not truly what they want to explore, or it is just an off-day.

18.9.2 Strategies to Try

- **Check the Question**: Is it the real issue or a placeholder? Sometimes people ask about career but are really worried about family.
- **Try a Different Spread**: Maybe a simpler approach will give clarity.
- **Offer a Re-Shuffle**: Suggest a fresh start. If they agree, shuffle again with a clear focus.
- **Acknowledge It**: "It seems we are not hitting the mark. It might be that the Tarot or we are not connecting today. That

is okay. Perhaps take some time, and we can try another day if you wish."

18.9.3 Respecting the Outcome

If it just is not working, do not force it. You can say, "Sometimes readings do not resonate right away. Feel free to come back later if anything changes." This honest approach is better than trying to invent something just to please them.

18.10 Self-Care After Difficult Readings

18.10.1 Emotional Reset

If you handle a reading that is intense—like topics of abuse, grief, or big life crises—take a moment afterward to breathe or stretch. Remind yourself that while you offered support, you are not responsible for solving all their problems. You gave them insight; the rest is up to them.

18.10.2 Clearing the Space

Some readers like to "clear" their reading space by tidying up the cards, maybe passing them through incense or lightly knocking on the deck to reset its energy (if that resonates with you). This ritual can help you mentally separate from the reading you just did, so you do not carry the stress into the next one.

18.10.3 Talking It Out (If Appropriate)

If a reading leaves you unsettled, you might confide in a mentor or a trusted Tarot-reading friend—without breaking the querent's anonymity or privacy details. For example: "I did a reading about someone dealing with deep grief, and I feel shaken. Any tips on how to cope?" This can help you process your feelings. Just be sure not to reveal the querent's personal information.

18.11 Practical Exercises to Strengthen Resilience

18.11.1 "What If" Scenarios

Role-play or imagine tricky scenarios. For instance, "What if a querent asks about a serious illness?" or "What if the cards completely contradict each other?" Write down how you would respond. This mental rehearsal makes you feel more prepared when challenges occur in real readings.

18.11.2 Spread Practice Under Pressure

Time yourself to do a quick 3-card reading in 5 minutes, forcing yourself to interpret swiftly yet clearly. Speed drills can help you stay calm under stressful real-life conditions—like a party setting where many people are waiting.

.18.11.3 Journaling Card Contradictions

Pull two random cards that look or feel opposite (e.g., The Sun vs. The Moon). Write a short paragraph on how they might coexist in one reading. This trains your brain to see unity in contrast, a key skill for puzzling readings.

Chapter 19: Advanced Methods and Techniques

19.1 Why Explore Advanced Methods?

By now, you know how to shuffle, lay out spreads, interpret symbols, and read for yourself or others. That is already a lot! But Tarot is like a large garden—you can keep finding new areas to explore. **Advanced methods** can include blending Tarot with other spiritual or creative tools, adding extra layers to your readings, or discovering ways to connect deeper with your inner self.

Perhaps you are curious about incorporating astrology or numerology, or you want to experiment with special rituals to enrich your readings. Or maybe you want to do "shadow work," which involves exploring parts of yourself you usually ignore or fear. This chapter will give you an overview of such methods and how they can expand your Tarot practice. Remember, there is no pressure to try everything. Pick what resonates with you, and always keep an open mind.

19.2 Combining Tarot with Other Tools

19.2.1 Astrology

Astrology involves planets, zodiac signs, and birth charts. Some advanced Tarot readers link each Major Arcana card to a zodiac sign or planet. For example, The Emperor might align with Aries (leadership, boldness), The Chariot with Cancer (determination, emotional strength), or The Star with Aquarius (hope, vision).

If you know your birth chart, you can look at which zodiac energies are strong and see how they might connect to Tarot. For instance, if your chart shows lots of fire signs (Aries, Leo, Sagittarius), you might feel drawn to the suit of Wands, which also represents fire. During a reading, you might say, "My strong Aries nature is showing up in The Emperor card." This can give fresh insight into how cosmic influences blend with your life themes.

19.2.2 Numerology

Numerology is the study of numbers and their symbolic meanings. In Tarot, each card in the Minor Arcana has a number (Ace through 10). Aces (1) can mean beginnings, 2 can mean partnership or duality, 3 can mean growth, 4 can mean stability, and so on. If you delve deeper into numerology, you might say, "The number 7 means introspection or spiritual search," so the 7 of Cups could highlight confusion or daydreaming tied to deeper self-searching.

You can also look at the sum of the digits in your birthdate to find a "life path number," then see how that number's energy appears in your readings. Numerology can make your interpretations more layered. For instance, if your life path number is 6, you might resonate strongly with the Lovers (Major Arcana VI) or the 6 of Wands, 6 of Cups, etc.

19.2.3 Crystals and Stones

Some people place **crystals** on their reading table—like amethyst for calm or clear quartz for clarity. You can set a crystal on top of a card that feels important. For example, if you are meditating on the High Priestess, you might place a moonstone next to it to enhance intuition. Or if you want to ground yourself while reading the Pentacles suit, you could hold a piece of hematite.

Crystals do not magically make your reading "better," but they can add a sense of ritual, focus, and beauty. Some readers feel crystals amplify certain energies. If that speaks to you, try it. If not, you can simply see them as decorative.

19.2.4 Oracle Cards or Runes

In addition to Tarot, there are many **oracle decks**—cards with messages or images that do not follow the 78-card Tarot system. Some readers pull an oracle card after a Tarot reading to get a final piece of advice or a theme word. You might do a spread and then draw one card from an angel oracle deck that says "Compassion" or "Forgiveness," giving you a hint about how to approach the reading's outcome.

Likewise, some advanced readers use **runes** (an ancient alphabet used for divination) alongside Tarot. They might draw a single rune to clarify a tricky card. If the rune for "joy" appears, maybe the confusion lifts, and you see a more positive angle in that card. Mixing divination tools can spark creativity and deeper reflection.

19.3 Rituals and Spiritual Practices

19.3.1 Creating a Sacred Space

We have talked about setting up a calm environment. **Advanced ritual** might include lighting certain colored candles for each suit (red for Wands, blue for Cups, yellow for Swords, green or gold for Pentacles) or using incense to mark the start and end of a reading session. Some readers arrange crystals in a circle around the reading table or recite a short poem or prayer to invite guidance.

These rituals are not about making Tarot "real." Tarot is already a valid tool whether you use rituals or not. Rather, they help you shift into a focused mindset. If you like the feeling of reverence, these practices can make your readings feel more significant. If you prefer a simple approach, that is also fine.

19.3.2 Moon Phases and Timing

Some advanced readers time their Tarot work with **moon phases**. For instance, a new moon can be a good time for spreads about beginnings or setting intentions, while a full moon might be for releasing or celebrating. You might do a monthly reading on the new moon to see what energies are emerging for the next four weeks.

Others pick special dates, like an equinox or solstice, for a more elaborate spread. The idea is to align with nature's cycles, feeling part of a bigger flow. This can add a sense of magic or synchronicity to your Tarot sessions.

19.3.3 Elemental Invocations

Some advanced Tarot practitioners connect each suit to its element (Wands = Fire, Cups = Water, Swords = Air, Pentacles = Earth) and call upon those energies before readings. For instance, you might say, "I call upon the warmth of Fire to ignite my creativity, the depth of Water to open my heart, the clarity of Air to sharpen my thoughts, and the stability of Earth to ground my insights."

This short invocation can remind you to stay balanced among all four elements. It is symbolic, not literal magic. But it can help you remember that each suit is a piece of the larger puzzle called life.

19.4 Advanced Spread Design

19.4.1 Multi-Layered Spreads

Instead of placing cards in a single row or circle, some advanced spreads layer positions on top of each other. For example, you might have a "Main Situation" row and then place a second row of "Underlying Influences" beneath it. Or you could do a spread that has an outer ring of cards for external factors (like friends, family, work) and an inner ring for personal emotions.

This layering can help you see different levels of a situation. For instance, the top card might show what is visible or obvious, while the card underneath might show hidden motives or subconscious feelings. Designing your own layered spread can be creative and reveal new angles.

19.4.2 Spiral or Mandala Layouts

Instead of the typical line or cross, you might arrange cards in a **spiral** or **mandala** shape. A spiral spread might start at the center with one card (core issue) and spiral outward with each ring representing a new phase or challenge. A mandala spread might place cards in four directions (north, east, south, west), each direction symbolizing something (like mind, body, heart, spirit).

Such spreads can visually remind you that life is cyclical or that multiple forces act at once. They can be more time-consuming to read because you have to keep track of how each position relates to the shape, but they can also offer a rich, holistic view.

19.4.3 Storytelling Spreads

If you love **storytelling**, you can create a spread where each card is a "chapter." Card 1 is "Once Upon a Time," card 2 is "Conflict," card 3 is

"Wise Mentor," card 4 is "Challenge," card 5 is "Climax," and card 6 is "Resolution." By framing your reading as a story, you might see your role as the hero or heroine facing conflicts and meeting allies or obstacles. This is great for creative folks or anyone who enjoys seeing their life as a narrative with arcs and lessons.

19.5 Deeper Psychological or Spiritual Work

19.5.1 Shadow Work

Shadow work is about exploring the parts of ourselves we usually hide—like fears, insecurities, or patterns we inherited but do not fully understand. In Tarot, you might do a spread to ask, "What am I repressing or avoiding?" or "What do I need to heal from my past?" You might see a "scary" card (like The Tower or The Devil) that indicates deep-seated issues.

Shadow work requires honesty. It can be emotional. You might discover anger you did not know you had, or realize you have been sabotaging yourself in certain relationships. The goal is not to judge yourself harshly but to bring those hidden parts to light so you can grow.

19.5.2 Inner Child Work

Another advanced approach is **inner child work**, where you connect with the younger version of yourself. You could pull a card asking, "What does my inner child want me to remember?" or "How can I bring more playfulness into my life?" If a card shows a scene of joy or innocence (like the Six of Cups), you might interpret it as a message to revisit childlike wonder. Or if The Moon appears, it might suggest hidden fears from childhood that still need healing.

19.5.3 Connecting with Spiritual Guides

Some readers believe in **spirit guides**, angels, or other helpful presences. If you do too, you can create a special spread to communicate with them. You might label each position: "Message from my guide," "What I need to learn right now," and "How to apply it." You can also hold a personal item (like a crystal or a piece of jewelry) while shuffling to feel more connected. If you are not comfortable with this idea, that is fine—Tarot is flexible, and you can stick to more practical or psychological approaches.

19.6 Working with Reversed Cards More Deeply

19.6.1 Refined Reversal Interpretations

We have mentioned **reversed cards**—those that appear upside down. Many advanced readers go beyond seeing reversals as just "the opposite meaning." They might interpret reversals as:

- **Blocked Energy**: The upright meaning is there, but not flowing smoothly.
- **Inner Focus**: Instead of external events, the reversed card points to internal processes.
- **Delay**: The card's lesson will come, but it is postponed or slowed.
- **Shadow Aspect**: The reversed version shows the card's "darker" side—like a reversed Empress indicating smothering rather than nurturing.

19.6.2 Selective Reversals

Some advanced readers do not automatically mix reversed cards into the deck. They might choose to reverse only a few cards intentionally, maybe 10-20% of the deck, so they feel each reversal is truly meaningful. Or they might only allow reversals in a certain spread about deep introspection. This selective approach can make reversals feel special and not just random.

19.7 Reading for Special Situations

19.7.1 Group or Party Readings

If you read at a party or group setting, advanced techniques might include using quick, fun spreads so you can read for multiple people. You could do a "Party Spread" with three cards: "Your vibe tonight," "A surprise ahead," and "Best way to have fun." Keep it light. If someone wants a deeper reading, you can step aside to a quieter spot.

19.7.2 Yearly or Seasonal Readings

You can do a **yearly reading** with 12 cards, each representing a month. Then add a 13th card as the "theme." Or do seasonal spreads—one for spring, summer, autumn, winter—pulling cards to see what energies might arise in each season. This helps you plan your goals or watch for potential challenges. People often revisit these spreads throughout the year to see how accurate or useful they are.

19.7.3 Dream Interpretation

If you have a vivid dream, you can **use Tarot to interpret** it. For instance, pick the card that best symbolizes your dream's main mood or conflict (like The Moon for mystery, or the Seven of Cups if the dream was filled with illusions). Shuffle the deck asking, "What message does this dream hold for me?" Pull a few cards and link them to dream symbols. This merges dream work with Tarot, often revealing subconscious insights.

19.8 Continuous Learning and Refinement

19.8.1 Advanced Study Resources

- **Books by Experienced Authors**: Some advanced Tarot books dive into deep symbolism, Qabalah, or historical references.
- **Workshops and Classes**: Live or online workshops can teach specialized areas, like Tarot for healing or Tarot for creativity.
- **Mentors or Tarot Circles**: Joining a local Tarot group or an online forum with advanced discussions can sharpen your skills. You can exchange ideas, ask for feedback on tricky spreads, or learn new techniques.

19.8.2 Personal Experiments

Part of advanced practice is **experimenting** on your own. Create new spreads, try reading under different conditions (like early morning vs. late night), track the results in a journal, and see what resonates. You might notice your readings feel more intuitive after meditating or that certain decks work better with certain spreads. Finding your unique style is half the fun.

Chapter 20: Growing as a Tarot Reader

20.1 The Lifelong Journey of Tarot

You have come a long way—from learning the basics of the 78 cards to exploring advanced methods in Chapter 19. Yet Tarot is not something you "finish" like a simple puzzle. It is more like a never-ending path with new discoveries around every bend. **Growing as a Tarot reader** is about continuing to practice, reflect, and evolve your style. You might find that your approach changes as you move through different life stages—what worked for you at 15 might feel different at 35 or 60. This chapter guides you in keeping the learning process active and enjoyable.

20.2 Tracking Your Progress

20.2.1 Journaling and Reflection

One of the simplest, most powerful ways to grow is by **keeping a Tarot journal**. Every time you do a reading—especially one that feels significant—write down:

- The date and time.
- The question or topic.
- The spread and which cards appeared.
- Your immediate interpretation.
- Any follow-up thoughts days or weeks later (did events happen as you sensed, or did you see new meanings over time?).

By reviewing old journal entries, you see how your understanding of cards has deepened or changed. You might notice that once you saw the Six of Pentacles as purely about money, but months later you realized it also applies to emotional give-and-take in relationships. This self-awareness shapes you into a thoughtful reader.

20.2.2 Milestones and Goals

It can help to set **small goals**. For instance:

- **Memorize** or get comfortable with all 78 cards in your chosen deck by a certain date.
- **Practice** reading for a friend once a week for a month.
- **Create** your own spread and test it out with three different situations.

When you reach a goal—like feeling confident reading for family gatherings—celebrate! This sense of achievement keeps you motivated to explore new levels.

20.2.3 Checking Accuracy and Resonance

Tarot is partly about synchronicity and personal growth, not just "accuracy." But if you want to gauge how often your interpretations resonate with real life, keep notes. Did your reading about a friend's job trouble match how events unfolded? Did the advice from your daily card help you? Accuracy is not everything—sometimes a "wrong" reading might spark needed reflection—but noticing patterns can sharpen your interpretive instincts.

20.3 Building Confidence and Consistency

20.3.1 Regular Practice

Just like learning a musical instrument or a sport, **practice** is key. You do not have to do huge spreads every day. Even small steps—like pulling a daily card—keep you connected. If you skip Tarot for months, you might feel rusty. Think of Tarot like a friend you visit often enough to stay in tune with each other.

20.3.2 Dealing with Self-Doubt

You might wonder, "Am I really any good at this?" or "What if I read a card incorrectly?" That is normal. Remember, Tarot is an art. Two readers can see the same card and highlight different aspects, and both can be valid. If you find self-doubt creeping in, revisit your successes—like times when your reading really helped someone or gave you personal insight. Also, talk to fellow Tarot enthusiasts; hearing their stories of doubt can make you realize it is common and surmountable.

20.3.3 Consistent Ethics

Growing as a Tarot reader also means **upholding your ethical standards**. If you decide never to read about legal or medical issues, for example, keep that boundary firm, even if someone tries to persuade you. Sticking to your values builds trust in yourself and from others. If you ever slip—like giving in to an unethical request—use it as a learning moment and reaffirm your boundaries.

20.4 Exploring New Decks and Styles

20.4.1 Collecting Decks

Many readers eventually **collect multiple Tarot decks**. Each deck has unique art and might emphasize different themes (fantasy, animals, cultural stories, etc.). Owning several decks can broaden your interpretation skills because you see new ways of depicting the same card. For example, the Five of Cups might show spilled cups near a river in one deck and a sorrowful figure in a desert in another deck. Both images might spark different ideas.

Collecting can be fun, but be mindful not to buy so many decks that you never truly connect with any of them. Sometimes, focusing on just a few favorites allows deeper familiarity. If you find a deck you do not love, you can trade or gift it to someone who might appreciate it more.

20.4.2 Switching Approaches

Maybe you started with the Rider-Waite-Smith (RWS) deck and a straightforward interpretive style. Over time, you might try the Thoth deck or a Marseille-style deck, which have different visuals and symbolic traditions. This shift challenges you to see the cards in new ways. Or you might decide to read only with minimalistic "pip" decks (where the Minor Arcana have simple suit symbols, not full pictures). Trying new styles can refresh your practice and test your adaptability.

20.4.3 Personal Deck Creation

Some advanced readers **design their own decks**, even if it is just for private use. Drawing or collaging images for each card can deepen your understanding. You might pick symbols that are personally meaningful—like a mountain near your hometown for The Fool's journey, or a family heirloom to represent Pentacles. Even if your art skills are humble, the act of creating is powerful. Each card becomes a reflection of your life story.

20.5 Sharing Tarot with Others

20.5.1 Reading for Friends and Family

Reading Tarot for your close circle can strengthen bonds. They might see a side of you they never knew—one that is intuitive, empathetic, and patient. However, remember potential biases (Chapter 18). Reading for people you know well might cloud your interpretations, so stay mindful of that. Also, ask if they truly want a Tarot reading and respect their boundaries if they do not.

20.5.2 Volunteering or Community Events

Some Tarot readers offer **free or donation-based readings** at community centers, charity fundraisers, or local fairs. This is a way to give back and also polish your skills. Meeting various people and hearing diverse questions can rapidly grow your reading abilities. If you do volunteer, set a comfortable time limit or a waiting list system so you do not burn out.

20.5.3 Professional Readings

You might reach a point where you feel ready to **offer paid readings**—either online, at a local metaphysical shop, or through word-of-mouth. This step requires clarity on pricing, scheduling, and ethical guidelines. You might create a simple website or social media page explaining your approach. If you do not want to go professional, that is fine. Growing as a reader does not require making money, but it is an option if you enjoy reading for others and want to dedicate more time to it.

20.6 Building a Personal Tarot Routine

20.6.1 Daily or Weekly Check-Ins

Consider establishing a routine. For example:

- **Morning Card**: Pull one card, write a quick note about how it might shape your day.
- **Weekly Spread**: Every Sunday, do a 3-card reading about the week ahead—challenges, advice, and a theme.
- **Monthly Overview**: At the start of each month, do a larger spread (5 or 7 cards) about your goals, obstacles, and likely outcomes.

These small habits keep Tarot integrated into your life without overwhelming you. You can adapt the schedule if daily is too frequent or if you prefer a monthly approach. The key is consistency.

20.6.2 Seasonal or Yearly Goals

When a new season or year begins, revisit your Tarot goals:

- Is there a certain card you want to meditate on?
- Do you want to learn more about Court Cards?
- Are you intrigued by reversed cards or advanced spreads?

Write these down and check your progress periodically. Maybe by the next equinox or solstice, you aim to experiment with five new spreads you designed yourself.

20.6.3 Keeping It Fun

If Tarot becomes a chore, step back and remind yourself why you loved it in the first place. Sometimes, we get too serious or fixated on perfect technique. You can do playful readings—like pulling cards to plan a fictional story or to get costume ideas for a party. Let your imagination roam. This sense of fun can spark new insights and keep your enthusiasm alive.

20.7 Reflecting on Personal Growth

20.7.1 Self-Awareness and Transformation

One of Tarot's gifts is how it helps you learn about yourself—your strengths, fears, patterns, and desires. As you grow with Tarot, you might notice you have become more compassionate or more patient in real life. You might communicate better because you have practice explaining card meanings. Or you might handle problems differently, drawing on the wisdom of cards like Strength or The Hermit. Acknowledge these positive changes. Tarot does not just read the future; it can shape who you are becoming.

20.7.2 Celebrating Progress

Once a year (maybe on your Tarot "anniversary"), do a special reading about how you have evolved. You can ask:

1. **What have I learned in the past year through Tarot?**
2. **What personal qualities have grown stronger?**
3. **What do I still need to work on or explore further?**

Seeing the shifts in your perspective or reading style can be inspiring. You might realize you are more confident giving advice or better at noticing small symbols in a card's background. These are real achievements worth celebrating.

20.7.3 Handling Plateaus

Sometimes, you might hit a **plateau**—a stretch of time when you feel you are not improving or your readings feel repetitive. This is normal in any skill. Try a fresh deck, a new spread, or a short break. Read a Tarot book by a different author to spark new ideas. Plateaus often lead to breakthroughs once you try something different or let yourself rest and return with fresh eyes.

20.8 Contributing to the Tarot Community

20.8.1 Online Forums or Groups

If you want to grow further, consider joining **online Tarot communities** where people share readings, deck reviews, or new spreads. You can post your own reading (removing personal info if needed) and ask, "What do you all see here?" or "How would you interpret these cards?" Many advanced readers enjoy helping newcomers or exchanging perspectives with peers.

20.8.2 Writing and Teaching

Once you feel comfortable, you could write articles or blog posts about your Tarot experiences. Or offer a small workshop in your local library on "Tarot for Beginners." Teaching is a fantastic way to deepen your own knowledge. You have to articulate your understanding clearly, which makes you examine each card and interpretive method. Even short videos or social media posts can let you share your insights while learning from feedback.

20.8.3 Deck and Book Reviews

If you love collecting decks and reading Tarot books, you might do **reviews**. Sharing what you like or dislike can guide others in finding resources that match their style. For instance, you might note that a certain deck's art is gentle and perfect for emotional readings, while another deck is bold and suits career questions well. Reviews help the community navigate the huge variety of Tarot materials out there.

20.9 Embracing the Tarot Mindset

20.9.1 Living the Cards

As you grow, you may notice Tarot concepts popping up in daily life. You might say, "I am having a Five of Wands day at work—everyone is arguing!" or "This feels like a Hermit weekend—I need solitude to reflect." Some readers enjoy seeing life through the lens of Tarot archetypes, naming energies as they appear. This can make you more mindful, turning everyday experiences into learning moments.

20.9.2 Bringing Compassion and Curiosity

The core of Tarot growth is **compassion (for yourself and others)** and **curiosity (about life's mysteries)**. Every reading, even if it seems trivial, is a doorway into someone's thoughts or your own. Approaching it with kindness—rather than judgment—and genuine interest keeps Tarot fresh and meaningful. If you ever catch yourself feeling bored or cynical, pause and reconnect with that sense of wonder.

20.9.3 Encouraging Others

If you see new learners, cheer them on. Remember what it was like when you first memorized the suits and the differences between Major and Minor Arcana. Offering a tip or a comforting word can make a big difference. Contributing positive energy to the broader Tarot community enriches everyone's journey.

20.10 Final Thoughts

Tarot is not just a set of cards; it is a companion that can walk with you through many phases of life. You can use it casually, for daily reflections or occasionally when big decisions loom. Or you can dive deeper, weaving it into a robust spiritual or creative practice. The choice is yours.

Growing as a Tarot reader means staying open to learning from your own experiences, from books and mentors, from the cards themselves, and from the people you read for. It is about balancing knowledge with intuition, discipline with play, and confidence with humility.

You might go through ups and downs: times of excitement and discovery, times of doubt or plateau. But if you stick with it, you will likely find Tarot remains a loyal ally, whispering stories and insights that help you better understand yourself, others, and the world.

www.ingramcontent.com/pod-product-compliance
Lightning Source LLC
LaVergne TN
LVHW012039070526
838202LV00056B/5545